Australia New Zealand Closer Economic Relations Trade Agreement (ANZCERTA) and Regional Integration

The **ASEAN Studies Centre** of the Institute of Southeast Asian Studies in Singapore is devoted to working on issues that pertain to the Association of Southeast Asian Nations as an institution and a process, as distinct from the broader concerns of the Institute with respect to Southeast Asia.

Through research, conferences, consultations, and publications, the Centre seeks to illuminate ways of promoting ASEAN's purposes — political solidarity, economic integration and regional cooperation — and the obstacles on the path to achieving them. Through its studies, the Centre offers a measure of intellectual support to the ASEAN member-countries and the ASEAN Secretariat in building the ASEAN Community, with its political/security, economic and socio-cultural pillars. The Centre aims to conduct studies and make policy recommendations on issues and events that call for collective ASEAN actions and responses.

The Centre seeks to work together with other intellectual centres, institutes, think-tanks, foundations, universities, international and regional organizations, government agencies, and non-governmental organizations that have similar interests and objectives, as well as with individuals scholars and the ASEAN Secretariat.

The **Institute of Southeast Asian Studies (ISEAS)** was established as an autonomous organization in 1968. It is a regional centre dedicated to the study of socio-political, security and economic trends and developments in Southeast Asia and its wider geostrategic and economic environment. The Institute's research programmes are the Regional Economic Studies (RES, including ASEAN and APEC), Regional Strategic and Political Studies (RSPS), and Regional Social and Cultural Studies (RSCS).

ISEAS Publishing, an established academic press, has issued more than 2,000 books and journals. It is the largest scholarly publisher of research about Southeast Asia from within the region. ISEAS Publishing works with many other academic and trade publishers and distributors to disseminate important research and analyses from and about Southeast Asia to the rest of the world.

ASEAN
Studies Centre
Institute of Southeast Asian Studies

Report No. 11

Australia New Zealand Closer Economic Relations Trade Agreement (ANZCERTA) and Regional Integration

Robert Scollay · Christopher Findlay · Uwe Kaufmann

ISEAS

INSTITUTE OF SOUTHEAST ASIAN STUDIES
Singapore

First published in Singapore in 2011 by
ISEAS Publishing
Institute of Southeast Asian Studies
30 Heng Mui Keng Terrace
Pasir Panjang
Singapore 119614
E-mail: publish@iseas.edu.sg
Website: bookshop.iseas.edu.sg

The responsibility for facts and opinions in this publication rests exclusively with the authors and their interpretations do not necessarily reflect the views or the policy of the publisher or its supporters.

ISEAS Library Cataloguing-in-Publication Data

Scollay, Robert.
    Australia New Zealand closer economic relations trade agreement (ANZCERTA) and regional integration / Robert Scollay, Christopher Findlay and Uwe Kaufmann.
    1. Australia—Commerce—New Zealand.
    2. New Zealand—Commerce—Australia.
    3. Australia—Foreign economic relations—New Zealand.
    4. New Zealand—Foreign economic relations—Australia.
    I. Findlay, Christopher C. (Christopher Charles)
    II. Kaufmann, Uwe.
    III. Title.
HF3948 N45S42   2011

ISBN 978-981-4279-97-0 (soft cover)
ISBN 978-981-4279-98-7 (e-book PDF)

Typeset by Superskill Graphics Pte Ltd
Printed in Singapore by

CONTENTS

FOREWORD

The ASEAN Studies Centre at the Institute of Southeast Asian Studies (ISEAS) has been casting an analytical eye on regional, intergovernmental associations elsewhere in the world. It has published a study on the Common Market of the South (MERCOSUR) made up of Argentina, Brazil, Paraguay, and Uruguay. The North American Free Trade Agreement, as well as the Association of Southeast Asian Nations, was a central focus of the ASEAN-Canada Forum that the Centre, with the support of the International Development Research Centre (IDRC), organized at ISEAS in November 2008. A summary of the proceedings of the forum and the papers presented at it have been published in hard copy and posted online on www.iseas.edu.sg/aseanstudiescentre. The Centre has commissioned a study on the Gulf Cooperation Council, and intends to commission one on the European Union.

These studies have several purposes. One is to satisfy our and others' curiosity about what is going on in other regions by way of regional association and cooperation. What are they doing that ASEAN can, but does not? What is ASEAN doing that they can, but do not? What can ASEAN learn from them, if anything? What can they learn from ASEAN, if anything? What are they really all about? What is their nature? What are their stated ambitions and their real purposes? What are their achievements thus far? Their failures? What in their histories and the characters of their peoples explain these? What are the political and social impulses that account for their successes — and shortfalls?

There is a more immediate, more pragmatic purpose to these studies. It is to be of use, in terms of background knowledge, to policymakers and negotiators, should they wish to make use of them. In any case, the studies are made available to them, even sent to them.

In the case of this particular study, we at the Centre thought that the economic integration between Australia and New Zealand, the Closer Economic Relations (CER), was exceptionally worth a close examination by ASEAN and its members. The relationship, anchored on the Australia New Zealand Closer Economic Relations Trade Agreement, or ANZCERTA, is characteristic of a free trade area seeking to bring down tariff and non-tariff barriers to trade, and otherwise create an integrated market between the two parties. It is not a customs union, which ASEAN does not aspire to be; each partner keeps its own tariff regime with respect to the outside world. It is hard-nosed, pragmatic, practical, realistic. And it is not less driven than ASEAN by domestic and international political imperatives.

Thus, we asked Robert Scollay, senior lecturer in the Economics Department of the University of Auckland, New Zealand, and Christopher Findlay, head of the School of Economics, University of Adelaide, Australia, to cast their trained eyes on the CER and evaluate the state of its progress and impact, its achievements and shortfalls, with the collaboration of Uwe Kaufmann.

In their very first sentence, the authors declare, "Economic integration between Australia and New Zealand ... is today widely regarded as a success story." They cite indicators as a measure of that success. No tariffs or quantitative restrictions impede trade between the two countries. (The ANZCERTA rules of origin are based on a 50 per cent regional value content requirement.) Anti-dumping actions against each other are no longer taken. There is a common government procurement market between them.

Trans-Tasman customs procedures have been streamlined. The two countries' competition and business laws are being harmonized. So are biosecurity laws and quarantine procedures. Product standards have been made compatible and mutual recognition arrangements concluded. Joint food standards have been adopted. An open skies air services regime prevails in the region. Only a few sectors, such as coastal shipping, are excluded from the agreement liberalizing trade in services. According to the authors, "Australians and New Zealanders (may) visit, live and work in each other's country without restrictions."

No investment agreement seeks to protect and attract investments from each other. The significance of this omission is often downplayed on the grounds that both economies have relatively open foreign investment policies, although recent Organization for Economic Cooperation and Development (OECD) research tends to challenge complacency on this score. The most that the two governments have committed to is the lowering of regulatory barriers to mutual investments and the costs to businesses of complying with them. Nor are there formal mechanisms to settle disputes between them on trade, investments, or other economic issues. Instead, the two governments seem to prefer bilateral consultations and dialogues for dealing with such disputes. They have not found it necessary or useful to set up an overarching supranational institution, preferring instead to put together *ad hoc* bodies to deal with specific issues as needed. There is apparently little interest in the adoption of a common currency and, therefore, in the need for the establishment of a common central bank, or for the convergence of macroeconomic policies. The steady unilateral reduction of Most Favoured Nation (MFN) tariffs by both countries undoubtedly diminished the potential for trade diversion arising from ANZCERTA, which was concluded in 1983. However, the overall results of empirical studies cannot be unequivocally said to support a conclusion that ANZCERTA has been trade creating, rather than trade diverting.

The authors attribute the success of the CER to several factors, some unique to Australia and New Zealand. The two countries have similar legal regimes. They both adhere to Western democratic values. Their peoples share the same origins. Cultural ties between them are strong. The free movement of people between them, which dates back to the 1840s and was formalized in the 1920s and strengthened by the adoption in 1973 of the Trans-Tasman Travel Arrangement (TTTA), helps cultivate a common identity, as well as support the integration of the trans-Tasman market. The federal-state relations in Australia make it relatively easy to include New Zealand in the arrangements governing those relations. The business sectors in both countries have supported, indeed pushed for, the integration measures. By the beginning of the 1990s, the framework for Australia-New Zealand economic integration was in place. Not least, the political leaderships of the two countries are fully committed to the economic-integration process, which has also been made possible by the economic reforms undertaken in both, including the liberalization of trade.

Not that the road to trans-Tasman economic integration has been smooth. There have been disputes, particularly in the early years of ANZCERTA, on a number of issues, including import licenses, exchange rates, subsidies, anti-dumping actions, and investments. There were also perceptions of ANZCERTA as trade diverting. The authors discuss these extensively.

The study concludes with a "tentative" listing of "possible lessons for ASEAN from the ANZCERTA experience". They emphasize the need for "(s)trong political support at the leadership level" and the "pursuit in both countries of wide-ranging economic-reform agendas". They call attention to the fact that Australia and New Zealand periodically set broad objectives rather than lay down detailed "blueprints", and instead engage in frequent consultation, dialogue, review, and joint study. They express their preference for the "pragmatic approach" of Australia and New Zealand to the pursuit of the objectives of economic integration, focusing on issues that the business communities in both countries consider as important. Part of this pragmatic approach is the avoidance of central supranational institutions in favour of joint institutions put together when called for to deal with specific issues. The settlement of disputes has been pursued largely through bilateral consultations rather than formal mechanisms. "Consultation with and pressure from the business sector in both countries" have been an "important factor" in economic integration (whereas such pressure has generally been absent in ASEAN).

RODOLFO C. SEVERINO
Head, ASEAN Studies Centre
Institute of Southeast Asian Studies
Singapore

AUSTRALIA NEW ZEALAND CLOSER ECONOMIC RELATIONS TRADE AGREEMENT (ANZCERTA) AND REGIONAL INTEGRATION

Executive Summary

Economic integration between Australia and New Zealand, with ANZCERTA as its central instrument, is today widely regarded as a success story. Tariffs and quantitative restrictions on bilateral trade in goods have been completely removed, trade in services between the two countries has been liberalized to a very large extent, and the citizens of both countries have long enjoyed the right to visit and work in each other's country without restriction. The absence of formal provisions for the liberalization of bilateral investment flows is usually qualified by noting that the basically open foreign investment policies of both countries facilitate a relatively free flow of investment between them, to the extent that Australia is the largest source of foreign direct investment into New Zealand, and New Zealand is the sixth largest source of foreign direct investment into Australia.

A single government procurement market has been established across the two countries. There has been very substantial progress in the harmonization or mutual recognition of standards and occupational qualifications. Customs procedures have been streamlined between the two countries. There is a substantial degree of cooperation on biosecurity matters. Anti-dumping actions on trade between the two countries have been abolished. There has been some degree of harmonization of competition law, and further harmonization of business law is being actively pursued.

Since 2004 both countries have been committed to the progressive establishment of a Single Economic Market (SEM).

The process of integration, stretching for just over forty years, with ANZCERTA having been in force for twenty-six of those years, has, however, been far from smooth and automatic. There were many hesitations and difficulties during the early years of the process, and it is only in the last twenty years that momentum towards economic integration could be said to have been continuously sustained. Even over this latter period there has been a degree of selectivity in the issues that the two governments have chosen to address as part of the economic integration agenda, and there have been variations over time in the pace at which the overall integration agenda, and individual issues within that agenda, have been pursued.

There are also some special features of the relations between Australia and New Zealand which have tended to facilitate economic integration between the two countries:

- A tradition of free movement of people between Australia and New Zealand dating back to early colonial times in the 1840s, and more recently formalized in 1973 by the establishment of the Trans-Tasman Travel Arrangement (TTTA). This "Arrangement" consists essentially of a series of ministerial understandings, duly reflected in immigration procedures in each country, that allow Australians and New Zealanders to visit, live, and work in each other's country without restriction. The free movement of labour thus pre-dates ANZCERTA by many years.
- Similar, though by no means identical, systems of law, based on common law.
- Australia's constitutional status as a federation, in which the federal or Commonwealth government shares powers over economic policy with the six Australian state

governments, has allowed some economic integration issues to be neatly resolved by agreement that, in effect, New Zealand should participate in arrangements already existing between the Australian state and federal governments.

- A strong traditional sense of community between the peoples of Australia and New Zealand, traceable in many ways to the common colonial heritage, and symbolized by the Australia and New Zealand Army Corps (ANZAC) tradition of military cooperation, despite more recent political differences, for example, over relationships with the United States.
- A shared interest in the 1980s in breaking away from policies based on import substitution, and the adoption of trade strategies oriented towards international competitiveness.

ANZCERTA came into force in 1983, replacing an earlier and relatively ineffective Free Trade Agreement (FTA) based on positive listing, dating from 1967. In its initial form ANZCERTA was a cautious, even timid agreement, with lengthy implementation periods and substantial "negative lists" of products not initially covered by the main liberalization provisions. This was a reflection of the very strong opposition faced by both governments to the lowering of manufacturing protection, especially in New Zealand. Taking into account the "negative lists" and the goods that were already traded duty-free between the two countries, this means that in practice no more than about 6 per cent of bilateral trade in manufactured goods between the two countries may have been immediately affected by ANZCERTA. An initial review of ANZCERTA was scheduled for 1988, five years after it came into force.

Investment was deliberately excluded from ANZCERTA, and the bilateral liberalization of services trade was not considered at that time.

Many difficulties arose during the early years of ANZCERTA, leading in some cases to considerable bickering between the parties. By the time of the 1988 review, however, the climate of opinion surrounding ANZCERTA had changed considerably, due to the adoption by both countries of programmes of unilateral Most Favoured Nation (MFN) tariff reduction as part of wider ranging processes of domestic reform, which were especially far-reaching in New Zealand's case. Subsequent liberalization and integration initiatives would be considerably facilitated by the ability of both governments to present them as natural complements to, or extensions of, processes of domestic reform that commanded a substantial degree of political consensus.

The changed atmosphere set the scene for the decisive steps that emerged as the outcome of the 1988 review, which would ensure the future evolution of ANZCERTA as an outward looking, trade creating agreement. The taking of these steps was driven in large measure by the political direction provided by the two prime ministers of the day. The developments that followed from the review may be summarized as follows:

•   Agreement was reached to accelerate the liberalization of goods trade dramatically, so that remaining tariffs and quantitative restrictions on all goods traded between the two countries, including those hitherto subject to "modified arrangements", were eliminated by 1990.

•   A CER Trade in Services Protocol providing for free trade in all services except for those inscribed by each country on their respective "negative lists". Both countries agreed to work towards the progressive removal of sectors from their "negative lists".

- A series of protocols and memoranda of understanding that provided the basis for work programmes on various dimensions of trade facilitation through the 1990s:
  - Memorandum of Understanding on Technical Barriers to Trade
  - Protocol on Harmonization of Quarantine Administrative Procedures
  - Joint Understanding on Harmonization of Customs Policies and Procedures
  - Memorandum of Understanding on Harmonization of Business Law
- Agreement to eliminate anti-dumping actions on trade between the two countries, with issues relating to fairness in trade to be addressed instead by the extension of competition law provisions in each country prohibiting abuses of market power to cover abuses that affect trans-Tasman trade in goods.
- Government procurement in both countries was opened up to free trans-Tasman competition through the inclusion of New Zealand in Australia's new National Preference Agreement on a zero-preference basis.

By the beginning of the 1990s, therefore, a framework for economic integration between Australia and New Zealand had been established that was sufficiently broad-based for it to become realistic to speak of the concept of a "single market" between Australia and New Zealand, although this would not be adopted as an official policy objective of the two governments until much later, in 2004. This framework has formed the basis for the integration agenda that the two governments have pursued since that time.

Free trade in goods had been established as the cornerstone of integration, and a substantial commitment had been made to the liberalization of services trade with a further commitment to work towards the incorporation into the liberalization provisions of those services initially excluded. Full labour mobility was already a given. Understandings had been reached that would form the basis of progressively deeper cooperation and/or integration in the areas of customs procedures, quarantine/ biosecurity, standards and conformance, and business law, including competition law. Working towards mutual recognition arrangements had been established as an objective. Anti-dumping actions had been eliminated in relation to trade between the partners, and a decisive step had been taken to establish a region-wide government procurement market.

Two elements of a conventional "single market" were missing, however. First, no progress had been made in formally liberalizing investment flows between the two countries. Taxation-related problems had emerged as potentially significant hindrances to trans-Tasman investment that would intermittently occupy the attention of both governments and business interests over succeeding years. It took several years before the possibility of a breakthrough in this area emerged. Second, no serious consideration had been given to the formation of a customs union, although at least one prominent academic commentator (Lloyd 1991) had recommended such a step. Dissatisfaction with the ANZCERTA rules of origin, principally on the New Zealand side, had emerged as an issue that would be the subject of inconclusive debate until a decisive step to change the rules was taken in 2006.

Further important steps towards deeper integration were taken during the 1990s in the areas of standards and conformance and mutual recognition of qualifications:

- Establishment of Joint Accreditation System of Australia and New Zealand (JAS-ANZ), a joint accreditation system providing for a harmonized approach to auditing and certification of quality management systems on the basis of international standards.
- Conclusion in 1995 of the Agreement on Establishing a System for Development of Joint Food Standards (the Australia New Zealand Food Authority (ANZFA) agreement), providing for the establishment of a joint regulatory agency, the Australia New Zealand Food Authority (ANZFA), and a process leading to the finalization of a joint Australia New Zealand Food Standards Code by 1999.
- Conclusion in 1996 of the Trans-Tasman Mutual Recognition Arrangement (TTMRA), covering both occupational qualifications and product standards. In principle the TTMRA means that a good which is legally able to be sold in one country will also be legally able to be sold in the other, and a person registered to practise an occupation in one country will be entitled to practise an equivalent occupation in the other. In practise, it is effectively an extension of the Mutual Recognition Agreement (MRA) already existing between the Australian federal and state governments.
- A Single Aviation Market agreement was eventually implemented in 1996, after a considerable amount of bilateral "turbulence" over aviation market issues, and was subsequently reinforced by an Open Skies Agreement in 2000.
- In 2000 a new Memorandum of Understanding on Business Law Coordination was concluded to supersede the 1988 MOU. A range of issues was singled out for early attention, including competition law, securities law, takeovers law, consumer protection law, electronic transaction law,

disclosure regimes, cross-border insolvency, and patent examination. Coordination, cooperation, and consultation between the competition agencies of the two countries have steadily grown over time

A notable feature of ANZCERTA and its associated arrangements, which continues to the present day, is the absence of any formal dispute settlement mechanisms. Disputes are expected to be resolved through consultations between the relevant officials and ministers from each country. If one of the parties has a grievance regarding compliance with provisions of the agreement, the other party is obliged to enter into consultations on the issue. If consultation fails to resolve the dispute, however, there is no further arbitration or adjudicatory procedure provided under the agreement to which the aggrieved party can have recourse. The only option for the aggrieved party in such cases is recourse to dispute settlement under international agreements to which both partners are signatory, such as the World Trade Organization (WTO). Obviously this can only apply if the issue under dispute is covered by an international agreement that contains a dispute settlement mechanism. An example of this occurred recently when New Zealand referred a long-running dispute with Australia over the export of apples to Australia for dispute settlement at the WTO.

Bilateral policy developments in relation to the movement of people have left in place the essential freedom of movement, but have sought to address consequential issues relating to entitlements to welfare benefits, state funded medical treatment and pensions, and the associated cost implications for the two governments, as well as the Australian Government's requirement for enhanced control over movements of people in and out of Australia.

In the early twenty-first century, developments in the trade architecture of the wider Asia-Pacific region, and in particular, the separate pursuit by Australia and New Zealand of bilateral FTAs with other partners, raised questions over the degree of priority the two countries would in future place on their bilateral relationship. Rather than allow the bilateral economic relationship to wither, however, they decided instead to try to rejuvenate it. This decision was encapsulated in the commitment by the two countries in 2004 to pursue the achievement of a Single Economic Market (SEM). This commitment has been followed by significant developments in a number of areas:

- In 2006 the two countries agreed on a major change in the ANZCERTA rules of origin, involving a switch to Change in Tariff Classification (CTC) as the principal basis for determining origin, with exporters retaining the option of using the old Regional Value Contents (RVC)-based rules for a further five years.
- Work on aligning elements of the business law of the two countries has taken on new impetus since the commitment to the SEM. This is especially the case in competition policy and law.

Interest in monetary union between the two countries has been confined almost entirely to New Zealand. Essentially two possibilities have been under consideration: dollarization, whereby the New Zealand government unilaterally adopts the Australian dollar as its currency, and a formal monetary union, whereby the two governments would jointly adopt a single currency with a single central bank and monetary policy. In the latter case, it is typically assumed that the single currency would, in practice, be the Australian dollar and that the Australian central bank would assume the role of central bank for both countries.

The typical conclusion from analysis of the monetary union issue is that neither the benefits nor the costs of monetary union are likely to be large for New Zealand. The fact that there has been no discussion to date on the possible constitution of a common central bank in the event of a monetary union, and no discussion of measures to promote convergence of the two macroeconomies, indicates that monetary union is not yet being considered as a serious possibility.

Empirical studies of the economic effects of ANZCERTA are surprisingly scarce, and the overall impressions derived from those that are available are surprisingly ambivalent.

An early study by Australia's Bureau of Industrial Economics (BIE) in 1989 concluded that ANZCERTA is a trade creating FTA, and noted also the strongly increasing trend within trans-Tasman trade of intra-industry trade, where adjustment costs are generally considered to be lower than in case of inter-industry trade. The BIE also conducted a forward looking analysis of the potential welfare effects of ANZCERTA, which concluded that completion of merchandise trade liberalization under ANZCERTA would deliver substantial gains in economic welfare to both partners.

Later studies, using the now widely used backward-looking econometric methodology known as gravity modelling, have delivered much more mixed assessments. These gravity modelling studies invariably produce results for ANZCERTA as one of a sample containing a number (sometimes a substantial number) of Preferential Trade Agreements (PTAs). The results for the sample as a whole are intended provide tentative answers to the general question of whether preferential trade agreements have typically been trade creating or trade diverting in practice.

Initial studies using the gravity modelling methodology have produced results for ANZCERTA that are consistent with the overall findings of these studies that PTAs have in practice been predominantly trade creating on a net basis, with positive trade creation effects on trade with members outweighing diversion of trade away from non-members.

This assessment was strongly challenged by a study carried out at the Australian Productivity Commission (APC) by Adams *et al.* (2003) using a methodology designed to overcome a number of flaws that they identified in earlier studies. In addition to employing significantly more sophisticated econometrics, Adams *et al.* took into account both the differences in the depth of liberalization achieved in the various PTAs in their sample, and the date on which each PTA entered into force, neither of which was taken into account in most previous studies.

In direct contradiction to the results from earlier studies, Adams *et al.* found that the majority of PTAs in their sample were trade diverting rather than trade creating, and their results for ANZCERTA are consistent with this finding. Specifically ANZCERTA was one of a number of high-profile PTAs, including North American Free Trade Agreement (NAFTA), the European Community/Union and MERCOSUR, which had been found to be trade creating in most previous studies, but were found to be trade diverting by Adams *et al.*

DeRosa (2007) set out to test the robustness of the findings of Adams *et al.* (2003). Using a methodology that followed Adams *et al.* in many respects, in particular, their recognition of variation among PTAs in depth of liberalization and in dates of entry into force, but with a larger sample of countries, DeRosa produced results for the sample of PTAs in Adams *et al.* (2003) using a number of different econometric specifications. He also produced

results for a much larger sample of PTAs, but in these cases
without allowing for differences in depth of liberalization or date
of entry into force. In all cases DeRosa produced results for both
total merchandise trade and total trade in manufactures.

In general DeRosa's experiments yield mixed conclusions in
relation to the trade creating and trade diverting properties of
PTAs in the two samples. While a significant number of PTAs are
assessed as trade diverting, most of the procedures used by DeRosa
produce findings of net trade creation for the majority of the
PTAs in either sample, in contrast to the finding of Adams *et al.*
that the overwhelming majority of PTAs in their sample are trade
diverting. In particular, most of the larger PTAs, such as NAFTA,
the European Union, MERCOSUR, and AFTA, which were found
to be trade diverting by Adams *et al.* appear almost invariably as
trade creating in DeRosa's results. In this light it is particularly
striking that ANZCERTA continues to show as a trade diverting
PTA in a significant proportion of DeRosa's results. This is
especially true of his results for total merchandise trade using the
same sample as Adams *et al.* (2003), where the index used to
reflect variations in depth of liberalization explicitly recognizes
that the depth of liberalization in ANZCERTA is greater than in
most other PTAs in the sample. The indication that ANZCERTA
has resulted in a diversion of exports away from non-members is
particularly strong.

If the results of Adams *et al.* and DeRosa are considered
together, the overall indication that ANZCERTA should be
considered as a trade diverting PTA is considerably stronger than
in the case of major PTAs that were found by Adams *et al.* to be
trade diverting, such as the European Union, NAFTA, MERCOSUR,
and ASEAN Free Trade Agreement (AFTA).

This is a somewhat surprising conclusion, given the conventional view of ANZCERTA as one of the most far-reaching and comprehensive PTAs in terms of its liberalization processes. There is something of a puzzle here, which may offer an avenue for further research.

Implications for the welfare effects of ANZCERTA are perhaps even more unsettling. A PTA found to be trade diverting on a net basis must necessarily be welfare reducing. The results of Adams *et al.* and DeRosa suggest that there is a not insignificant probability that this is the case with ANZCERTA. Even if ANZCERTA were shown to be trade creating on a net basis, this would not guarantee that it must be welfare enhancing, as explained earlier.

Adams *et al.* also apply their methodology to an analysis of the impact of ANZCERTA on the investment flows of the two partners. They distinguish between the impact of trade and non-trade measures. The impact of the trade measures on investment is found to be weak and generally negative. The non-trade measures are found to have a negative effect on intra-PTA investment flows and on inward flows from non-members, but these effects are outweighed by a strong positive effect on outward flows to non-members, so that the overall effect is one of investment creation. Adams *et al.* qualify their results by noting that they may not be reliable.

To conclude, the following are tentatively put forward as possible lessons for ASEAN from the ANZCERTA experience:

1. Strong political support at the leadership level has been vitally important in sustaining the momentum of the integration process. This has been especially true in propelling the process across important thresholds, such as

the "breakthrough" represented by the 1988 Review and subsequent periods of transition from "flat" to "progressive" periods in the process.

2. The pursuit in both countries of wide-ranging economic reform agendas, including strong commitments to unilateral trade liberalization, facilitated political acceptance of individual integration initiatives, which could often be presented as natural extensions of the domestic reform process.

3. The periodic setting of objectives by leaders for the integration process has been important. Objectives were specified in broad terms rather than as detailed "blueprints" and were accompanied by the establishment of processes of consultation, dialogue, review, and joint study that helped to sustain the momentum of the process in the succeeding years.

4. A strongly pragmatic approach to the pursuit of the objectives was taken, focusing on issues that were highlighted as important to the business sectors of both countries or that were otherwise identified as impediments to integration for which practically and politically feasible solutions could be anticipated. Issues that were seen to raise severe political difficulties or sensitivities tended to be avoided, especially if the economic pay-off from addressing them was not seen to be substantial.

5. A pragmatic approach was also taken to institutional development. Supranational institutions were avoided. Joint institutions were established where considered necessary or desirable, to facilitate the implementation of new initiatives that were agreed upon from time to time by the parties, rather than in accordance with any pre-determined blueprint.

6. In the absence of a formal dispute settlement process, dispute resolution relies on consultative processes involving ministers and officials. This approach appears to be preferred by the parties and has generally worked reasonably well. There have been cases, however, where recourse to a robust dispute settlement process might have facilitated the early resolution of issues which, in the event, continued as irritants to the relationship for many years.

7. Consultation with and pressure from the business sector in both countries were an important factor in prioritizing the steps to be taken in pursuing deeper integration. Pressure that emanated from the business sector in only one of the two countries was less successful in securing changes.

8. The potential for trade diversion and consequent resource misallocation arising from the necessarily discriminatory character of an agreement such as ANZCERTA has been a theme in several assessments of ANZCERTA by professional economists. Ongoing unilateral trade liberalization of MFN tariffs by both partners has significantly reduced the scope for such distortionary effects. Nevertheless, empirical research has not been able to establish definitively that ANZCERTA is a trade creating rather than trade diverting FTA.

9. Even in countries with similar legal and regulatory systems, significant obstacles can be encountered in efforts to harmonize or reach agreement on some important areas of policy and law.

10. Even in a well established integration process, external shocks can create new challenges in apparently settled areas of policy.

ANZCERTA AND REGIONAL INTEGRATION

1. Introduction

Economic integration between Australia and New Zealand, with the Australia New Zealand Closer Economic Relations Trade Agreement (ANZCERTA) as its central instrument, is today widely regarded as a success story. Tariffs and quantitative restrictions on bilateral trade in goods have been completely removed, trade in services between the two countries has been liberalized to a very large extent, and the citizens of both countries have long enjoyed the right to visit and work in each other's country without restriction. The absence of formal provisions for the liberalization of bilateral investment flows is usually qualified by noting that basically open foreign investment policies in both countries facilitate a relatively free flow of investment between them, to the extent that Australia is the largest source of foreign direct investment into New Zealand and New Zealand, is the sixth largest source of foreign direct investment into Australia.

A single government procurement market has been established across the two countries. There has been very substantial progress in the harmonization or mutual recognition of standards and occupational qualifications. Customs procedures have been streamlined between the two countries. There is a substantial degree of cooperation on biosecurity matters. Anti-dumping actions on trade between the two countries have been abolished. There has been some degree of harmonization of competition law, and further harmonization of business law is being actively pursued.

Since 2004 both countries have been committed to the progressive establishment of a Single Economic Market (SEM). The process of integration, stretching for just over forty years, with ANZCERTA having been in force for twenty-six of those years, has however been far from smooth and automatic. There were many hesitations and difficulties during the early years of the process, and it is only in the last twenty years that momentum towards economic integration could be said to have been continuously sustained. Even over this latter period there has been a degree of selectivity in the issues that the two governments have chosen to address as part of the economic integration agenda, and there have been variations over time in the pace at which both the overall integration agenda, and individual issues within that agenda, have been pursued.

2. Background

There are a number of characteristics of Australia and New Zealand, and the relations between them, that are important for an understanding of the economic integration achieved through ANZCERTA and subsequent developments.

Constitutional and Legal Issues

The common origin of Australia and New Zealand as former colonies of Britain means that both countries have similar, though by no means identical, systems of law, based on common law.

Both countries are long-established democracies, with strong democratic institutions.

Australia is a federation, in which the federal or Commonwealth government shares powers over economic policy with the six Australian state governments. New Zealand does not have a state level of sub-national government. There is provision in the Australian constitution for the North Island and South Island of New Zealand to join the Australian federation as separate states, but there has not been any serious discussion on exercising this option, at least in recent times, although New Zealand commentators occasionally speculate about the possibility and potential merits of political union with Australia.

Social and Political Links

There has traditionally been a strong sense of community between the peoples of Australia and New Zealand, traceable in many ways to the common colonial heritage, and symbolized by the ANZAC tradition of military cooperation that remains revered in both countries. Divergent immigration policies in the last several decades have led to a significant difference in the ethnic composition of the two populations, and this in turn has tended to dilute the sense of community, which nevertheless remains an important factor in bilateral relations.

There has been political divergence as well, most notably in relations with the United States, with New Zealand's adoption of a "no nuclear" policy in the 1980s leading to the effective suspension of the Australia, New Zealand and United States Security (ANZUS) Treaty, and more recently the sharply divergent approach of the two countries towards support for the Iraq War. Australia has often been sharply critical of what it views as inadequate levels of defence expenditure by New Zealand, seeing this as "free riding" by New Zealand on Australia's much more substantial defence effort. Despite these differences, the governments in both countries have traditionally placed a high priority on strong bilateral political relations. This was clearly illustrated by the two immediate past prime ministers, John Howard and Helen Clark, who differed enormously in political orientation, world view, and personality, but nevertheless worked hard and consistently at maintaining and strengthening the political relationship.

Trade and Trade Policy

The global exports of both countries have been dominated by primary commodities — agricultural, forestry, and fisheries products in both countries, and minerals in the case of Australia. Nevertheless for some forty years or more from the Great Depression of the 1930s, both countries followed import substitution policies in defiance of their obvious comparative advantage, to the extent that by the 1970s the two countries had become distinguished for the highest levels of manufacturing protection in the OECD. The development of economic integration between Australia and New Zealand has been closely bound up with efforts, hesitant at first, to reduce the level of manufacturing protection, and the exports of Australia and New Zealand to each other have been dominated by manufactured goods, in sharp contrast to the pattern of global exports of each country.

Movement of People

Free movement of people between Australia and New Zealand dates back to early colonial times, in the 1840s. Formalization of this situation began with the development of reciprocal travel arrangements in the 1920s, followed in 1973 by the establishment of the Trans-Tasman Travel Arrangement (TTTA). This "Arrangement" consists essentially of a series of ministerial understandings, duly reflected in immigration procedures in each country, that allow Australians and New Zealanders to visit, live, and work in each other's country without restriction. For many years no passport was required for Australian and New Zealand citizens visiting each other's country, but in more recent times a valid passport has been required, and other policy provisions have been introduced in relation to welfare entitlements and pensions.

3. Pre-ANZCERTA Trade Arrangements

A New Zealand Australia Free Trade Agreement (known at the time as NAFTA) was established in 1967. This was a "positive list" agreement, in which the tariff reduction and elimination schedules applied only to an agreed list of products on each side. A process of regular consultations was established for adding further products to the lists of those covered by the agreement. This process quickly degenerated to the point where the consultations were involving the expenditure of large amounts of bureaucratic time and resources for the achievement of minimal gains in terms of increased product coverage of the agreement. A consensus developed that a fresh start was required if the two countries were to be serious about liberalizing trade with each other, and this led in turn to the establishment of ANZCERTA in 1983.

4. Early Years of ANZCERTA

Consistent with the desire to make a fresh start, ANZCERTA was a "negative list" agreement, in contrast to the "positive list" approach of its predecessor agreement. In its initial form, however, ANZCERTA was a cautious, even timid agreement. This was a reflection of the very strong opposition faced by both governments to the lowering of manufacturing protection, especially in New Zealand. The "negative list" consisted of a large number of manufactured products subject to "modified arrangements". In some cases the modification was designed to accommodate industry plans in one or both countries, either by lengthening the timetable for phasing out trade restrictions on the products concerned or by deferring the commencement of the phasing out of trade restrictions until an industry plan could be finalized. In other cases exceptions were made to allow the continuation of existing support schemes and trade restrictions. Special arrangements for some sensitive agricultural products (dairy products, wheat, sugar and tobacco) in effect constituted forms of "managed trade".

For products not subject to the "modified arrangements", tariffs were to be phased out over a five-year period ending in 1988, while quantitative restrictions (that is, restrictions imposed by New Zealand's import licensing system) were to be phased out over a twelve-year period, with special "Australia only" import licenses to be made available in annually increasing levels in order to permit progressive increases in the level of imports from Australia. Export incentives applying to bilateral trade were to be phased out by 1987. No attempt was made to create a customs union. There were significant differences in the tariff structures of the two countries at this time. For example, New Zealand typically allowed duty-free and quota-free entry of intermediate goods used as inputs in its manufacturing industries, ostensibly with the aim of promoting efficient manufacture in those industries, and apparently in blissful ignorance of the very high resulting rates of effective protection, with their obvious implications of very inefficient resource use. Australia, on the other hand, was concerned about promoting the domestic production of intermediate as well as finished goods, applied protective tariffs to imports of some intermediate as well as finished goods.

The rules of origin under ANZCERTA were based on a 50 per cent regional value content (RVC) rule.

Australia's Bureau of Industry Economics calculated that the "modified arrangements" covered some 44 per cent of bilateral

trade in manufactured goods, while a further 50 per cent of that
trade was already duty-free at the time ANZCERTA entered into
force (BIE 1989). The share of bilateral trade in manufactured
goods immediately affected by ANZCERTA was thus quite small.
The Bureau did report however that trade in this relatively small
group of immediately affected products did grow rapidly following
ANZCERTA coming into force.

Investment was deliberately excluded from ANZCERTA.
Australia objected that under its so-called "Nara Treaty"[1] with
Japan, any liberalization in favour of New Zealand investment
into Australia would have to be passed on to Japan as well.

The first five years of ANZCERTA's operation[2] were marked
by a considerable amount of bickering between the two partners.
Australian exporters were frustrated by perceived hindrances in
the way the "Australia only" import licenses operated and
complained of an unfair competitive advantage accruing to their
New Zealand rivals following a 20 per cent devaluation of the
New Zealand dollar. New Zealand interests became alarmed at
the growing use by Australia of "bounties" (essentially, production
subsidies) to compensate a number of key industries for reductions
in tariff protection. Continuation of some industry support schemes
and subsidies in both manufacturing and agriculture provided
another source of friction. Reaching agreement on full incorporation
into ANZCERTA of the sectors subject to "modified arrangements"
proved difficult. There was a substantial increase in anti-dumping
actions between the two countries. The early years of ANZCERTA
also saw some acrimonious disputes over investment issues; for
example, the refusal by Australia to allow New Zealand investment
in its banking sector.

From an economic perspective the relatively high MFN
tariffs applied by both countries to manufactured imports from

the rest of the world suggested substantial potential for welfare reducing trade diversion effects. There were also some well publicized cases of trade deflection (goods originating in a third country entering one partner for subsequent duty-free export to the other partner after minimal processing), and production deflection (for example Australian manufacturers transferring operations to New Zealand in order to benefit from duty-free access to intermediate inputs).

On a more positive note, ANZCERTA is credited with contributing to a change in the climate of opinion in both countries, but especially in New Zealand, towards reducing manufacturing protection, as manufacturers found they could survive and even prosper under ANZCERTA (Scollay 1996). This helped to lessen the intensity of opposition faced by the governments in both countries when they each subsequently moved unilaterally to phase down gradually the levels of their MFN tariffs. In New Zealand's case this policy change involved a decision to abandon entirely its import licensing system (the last elements of which finally disappeared in 1992), with the role of principal instrument of protection being allocated instead to tariffs, which themselves were to be phased down according to a pre-announced timetable. This was part of a sweeping programme of reform implemented by the New Zealand governments of the day in the late 1980s and early 1990s, which took advantage of a unique set of political circumstances.

With this move to unilateral liberalization by both countries, some of the difficulties that beset ANZCERTA in its early years either disappeared (for example, "Australia only" licenses were no longer necessary once New Zealand decided to abandon its import licensing system) or began to appear much more tractable (for example, the case for the "modified arrangements" appeared much less compelling). Unilateral reductions in MFN tariffs also reduced the potential for trade diversion as well as the scope for production and trade deflection. The scene was in effect set for decisive steps that would ensure the future evolution of ANZCERTA as an outward-looking, trade-creating agreement.

5. Consolidation of ANZCERTA

These decisive steps emerged as the outcome of the first major scheduled review of ANZCERTA in 1988, and were driven in large measure by the political direction provided by the two prime ministers of the day.[3]

Trade in Goods

Agreement was reached to accelerate dramatically the liberalization of goods trade, so that remaining tariffs and quantitative restrictions on all goods traded between the two countries, including those hitherto subject to "modified arrangements", were eliminated by 1990. A partial solution was agreed to New Zealand's concern over Australian "bounties", whereby "bounties" would not be paid to Australian manufacturers on exports to New Zealand, although New Zealand exporters to Australia continued to suffer from the effect of the "bounties" in offsetting their preferential access to the Australian market.

A number of new measures or initiatives designed to facilitate further free trade in goods were also agreed at this time. A Memorandum of Understanding on Technical Barriers to Trade, a Protocol on Harmonization of Quarantine Administrative Procedures, and a Joint Understanding on Harmonization of Customs Policies and Procedures launched work programmes that would progressively deepen cooperation and harmonization in each of these areas.

Elimination of Anti-Dumping — First Steps on Competition and Business Law

A ground breaking development was the agreement to eliminate anti-dumping actions on trade between the two countries. Issues relating to fairness in trade would be addressed instead by the extension of competition law provisions in each country prohibiting abuses of market power to cover abuses that affect trans-Tasman trade in goods. In order to give effect to this agreement changes were made to the relevant legislation in each country, including provision for the courts in each country to hear evidence relating to contraventions of these prohibitions in the other jurisdiction. Also in 1988 the two governments concluded a Memorandum of Understanding on Harmonization of Business Law, committing themselves to work towards identifying and pursuing potential areas for harmonization in this field.

Trade in Services

At this time also a new dimension was added to ANZCERTA through agreement on the CER Trade in Services Protocol providing for free trade in all services except for those services inscribed by each country on its "negative list". Both countries agreed to work towards the progressive removal of sectors from their "negative lists". This was an important stipulation, given that the "negative lists" included some of the sectors with the greatest potential for increased trade: both countries inscribed airways and air services, radio, television, telecommunications, postal services, and coastal shipping, while Australia also inscribed banking, health services, third-party insurance, construction, and engineering consultancies.

The CER Trade in Services agreement is a pre-GATS (General Agreement on Trade in Services) agreement and does not use some of the terminology that has become familiar from the latter agreement. Market access and national treatment rights are defined very broadly and simply in terms of a requirement for each partner to accord service providers of the other partner with access rights and treatment no less favourable than those accorded to their own providers. Unlike in General Agreement on Trade in Services (GATS), no definitions are provided of market access limitations that are thereby proscribed, although the agreement does enshrine the right of providers from each partner to choose their preferred form of commercial presence in the other partner. Another point of difference from GATS is that the partners are not permitted to schedule any limitations on their market access or national treatment commitments in relation to the services, other than those inscribed on their negative lists. On the other hand there is a significant limitation on the degree of liberalization of rights of establishment provided by the CER services agreement, in that the entire agreement applies, subject to the foreign investment policies of the two partner countries, which were at the time not and are still not, covered by ANZCERTA or its associated instruments. Movement of natural persons, however, which is often subject to the most restrictive liberalization provisions in other agreements, is completely unrestricted in the CER case under the Trans-Tasman Travel Arrangements (TTTA).

There is a "best endeavours" provision in the CER Trade in Services Agreement whereby mutual recognition of qualifications is encouraged. Each partner is also expected to ensure that licensing and certification procedures do not operate in a discriminatory fashion to withhold licensing or certification from providers of the other partner. The introduction or expansion of export subsidies, export incentives, and other measures with similar distortionary effects is banned. The partners committed themselves to working towards the elimination of existing measures of this type by mid-1990. Another "best endeavours" provision obliges the partners to seek to prevent state controlled service providers from using revenues derived from monopoly activities to cross-subsidize other activities in which they compete with other providers.

Government Procurement

Government procurement in both countries was opened up to free trans-Tasman competition through the inclusion of New Zealand in Australia's new National Preference Agreement on a zero preference basis. This was originally an Australian domestic arrangement designed to ensure that procurement by both federal and state governments in Australia would be open to free competition among all Australian suppliers. Extending this arrangement to include New Zealand was a logical way to liberalize government procurement between the two countries.

Overall Achievement: Framework for Integration in Place

By the beginning of the 1990s, therefore, a framework for economic integration between Australia and New Zealand had been established that was sufficiently broad-based for it to become realistic to speak of the concept of a "single market" between Australia and New Zealand, although this would not be adopted as an official policy objective of the two governments until much later, in 2004. This framework has formed the basis for the integration agenda that has been pursued by the two governments since that time.

Free trade in goods had been established as the cornerstone of integration, and a substantial commitment had been made to liberalization of services trade, with a further commitment to work towards incorporating into the liberalization provisions those services initially excluded. Full labour mobility was already a given. Understandings had been reached that would form the basis of progressively deeper cooperation and/or integration in the areas of customs procedures, quarantine/biosecurity, standards and conformance, and business law, including competition law. An objective of working towards mutual recognition arrangements had been established. Anti-dumping actions had been eliminated in relation to trade between the partners, and a decisive step had been taken to establish a region-wide government procurement market.

However, two elements of a conventional "single market" were missing. First, no progress had been made in formally liberalizing investment flows between the two countries. Taxation related problems had emerged as potentially significant hindrances to trans-Tasman investment that would intermittently occupy the attention of both governments and business interests over succeeding years. Second, no serious consideration had been given to the formation of a customs union, although at least one prominent academic commentator (Lloyd 1991) had recommended such a step. Dissatisfaction with the ANZCERTA rules of origin, principally on the New Zealand side, had emerged as an issue that would be the subject of inconclusive debate until a decisive step to change the rules was taken in 2006.

The high cost of trans-Tasman shipping, an issue which had been high on the list of concerns of both governments and business from the earliest days of integration efforts, continued to command attention, but without any agreement being reached on concerted action by the two governments. A central element in the issue was limitations on competition, linked in turn to an accord between

---

BOX 1[4]

Investment and ANZCERTA

ANZCERTA does not include an investment chapter nor is there any specific chapter or specific provisions on investment in the Services protocol (established in 1988), even though it is a "negative list" agreement. Both countries have pre-establishment screening processes for FDI, which covers trans-Tasman investment, as well as investment from other parties. The two relevant agencies are the Australian Foreign Investment Review Board and the New Zealand Overseas Investment Commission.

Table 1 — Liberalization of investment under Australia's FTAs

Feature	ANZCERTA	Australia-United States FTA	Australia-Chile FTA	Singapore-Australia FTA	Thailand-Australia FTA
Negative listing of investment chapter	No chapter	√	√	√	Positive
Broad definition of investor and investment	No definition	√	√	√	IMF definition
National treatment and MFN pre- and post-establishment	Services investors	√	√	NT only	√ limited to covered investments
Higher thresholds for screening and approval	x	√	x	x	X
Employment in investments + movement business persons	√ Free movement under TTTA	√ Senior management only	√	√	√

Feature	ANZCERTA	Australia-United States FTA	Australia-Chile FTA	Singapore-Australia FTA	Thailand-Australia FTA
Prohibition on performance requirements	x	√	√	x	x
Minimum standards for investment protection	x	√	√		√
Free transfers	x	√	√	√	√
Expropriation and compensation	x	√	√	√	√
Investor state dispute settlement	x		√	√	√

Source: Bondietti (2008)

Notes: √ indicates commitment x indicates absence of commitment

"Inconsistencies in Treatment of Foreign Investment in Trade Agreements", Australian APEC Study Centre, Monash University, December 2008, available at <http://www.apec.org.au/docs/08_AASC_IFDI.pdf>

Table 1 summarizes the current status of liberalization of investment in Australia's FTAs with New Zealand, the United States, Singapore, Chile, and Thailand.

ANZCERTA is an outlier among these FTAs in not including an investment chapter or any specific provisions on investment in the services protocol to ANZCERTA. The latter protocol includes obligations pertaining to direct investment by service providers, but these are subject to the foreign investment policies of the two countries.[5] The protocol thus confers additional post-establishment rights, but no additional pre-establishment rights on service investors. Bondietti (2008) finds that, even though the screening may be liberal, there is no right or guarantee of preferential legal treatment.

A tendency towards complacency regarding the lack of investment provisions in ANZCERTA-based on the "conventional wisdom" that the foreign investment policies of both countries are sufficiently liberalize as not to pose any serious hindrance in practice to trans-Tasman investment — is called into question by a recent OECD study.[6] The study examined measures of regulatory restrictions on inward foreign investment for twenty-nine OECD countries and thirteen non-OECD countries. On the aggregate restrictiveness index used in the OECD study, Australia emerged as the fifth most restrictive country among all countries in the study, and the second most restrictive among OECD members, while New Zealand was the fifteenth most restrictive overall, and the tenth most restrictive among OECD members. When the index is disaggregated into operational, screening, and equity requirement factors, Australia's restrictiveness score is relatively high for all three components, while New Zealand's restrictiveness score is especially high for screening requirements. When restrictiveness is broken down by sector, Australia's transport sector is the most restricted in the OECD, and the second most restricted overall. In the telecoms sector Australia has the highest restrictiveness score and New Zealand the fourth highest restrictiveness score among OECD countries in the study.

Impediments to trans-Tasman investment were addressed in 1999 in the Joint Prime Ministerial Task Force on Australia New Zealand Bilateral Economic Relations. This ultimately resulted in plans to liberalize and deepen further the Australia-New Zealand economic relationship by including investments in ANZCERTA.[7] In February 2006, the Australian and New Zealand Governments "agreed to commence the negotiation of an investment protocol to form part of ANZCERTA". In March 2009, both prime ministers committed themselves to finalize an investment protocol to lower the regulatory barriers and compliance costs to businesses with the goal of further promoting investments between the two economies.

"Any obstacles remaining in the investment fields and other fields, we're determined to punch our way through and we've talked about a couple of practical measures where we can take that work forward [...]."[8]

the maritime labour unions in the two countries. Progress on this issue would eventually be driven by domestic policy action in each country.

A notable feature of ANZCERTA and its associated arrangements which continues to the present day is the absence of any formal dispute settlement mechanisms. Disputes are expected to be resolved through consultations between the relevant officials and ministers from the two countries. If one of the parties has a grievance regarding compliance with provisions of the agreement, the other party is obliged to enter into consultations on the issue. If consultation fails to resolve the dispute however there is no further arbitration or adjudicatory procedure provided under the agreement to which the aggrieved party can have recourse. The only option for the aggrieved party in such cases is recourse to dispute settlement under international agreements to which both partners are signatory, such as the WTO. Obviously this can only apply if the issue under dispute is covered by an international agreement that contains a dispute settlement mechanism.

6. Deepening Integration

The period since the early 1990s has seen the further formalization and deepening of economic integration between the two countries across the broad range of issues covered in the integration framework that had been established at the end of the preceding decade. Much of this progress involved programmes and processes developed to give effect to the commitments to further cooperation arising from understandings reached in the 1988 review and its immediate aftermath. In other cases the governments responded to newly emerging problems or to pressure from the business communities in one or both countries.

The level of priority given by the two governments to trans-Tasman economic integration tended to vary over time. Lloyd

(1995) notes that some variation in the prioritization of issues was related to domestic politics in each country. He also notes that pressure for further deepening of integration tended to emanate more from the New Zealand side, whereas the Australian Government was more inclined to be content with the level of integration already achieved. He relates this to the obvious fact that the relationship is of much greater relative importance to New Zealand than to Australia, so that New Zealand would generally tend to see greater gains from further integration. Against this background the maintenance of momentum owed much to the intensive programme of regular meetings established between various groups of officials and ministers to give effect to the understandings reached between the two governments, as well as the formal reviews of ANZCERTA which took place, for example, in 1992 and 1995.

Trade in Goods: Rules of Origin

Difficulties with the ANZCERTA rules of origin, especially on the New Zealand side, were a frequent subject for discussion. As a result the rules were modified in ways designed to provide some additional flexibility, but the 50 per cent RVC requirement remained the basis of the rules. Inability to reach agreement on a substantial lowering of the RVC requirement was said to be a contributing factor to the closure of the New Zealand motor vehicle assembly industry in 1998 (Scollay *et al.* 1998).

Customs

The Joint Understanding on Harmonization of Customs Policies acted as a springboard for sustained cooperation between the customs administrations of the two partners, streamlining and simplifying customs procedures applying to bilateral trade, and harmonizing procedures where considered appropriate. The original Understanding was reinforced in 1996 by the conclusion of Cooperative Arrangements Regarding Mutual Assistance between Customs administrations. The degree of confidence and trust between the two administrations has facilitated a number of arrangements to exchange information, for example, exchange of risk and threat analyses, exchange of commercial shipping risk assessments where the next port of call is in the other partner, and operational intelligence sharing in relation to air passenger stream.

Quarantine/Biosecurity

The Protocol on Harmonization of Quarantine Administrative Procedures has also led to substantial progress on harmonization of quarantine procedures. A high-level dialogue known as the Consultative Group on Biosecurity Cooperation (CGBC) was established in 1999 to examine procedures further, particularly risk analysis procedures, with a view to streamlining them, as well as regularly reviewing other aspects of the biosecurity interaction between the two countries. The CGBC has four working groups dealing with plant health, animal health, border operations, and risk analysis.

The Protocol also provided for joint efforts to resolve specified outstanding quarantine issues impeding bilateral trade in goods. The majority of these were successfully resolved. The dispute over the export of New Zealand apples to Australia could not, however, be resolved by consultation, and no bilateral mechanism exists for adjudication on the issue. New Zealand eventually decided to refer this dispute to the WTO's dispute settlement process.

BOX 2
Case Study: Apple Dispute between Australia and New Zealand

The dispute over New Zealand's apple exports to Australia provides a good example of how these two highly integrated trading partners may be unable to resolve certain trade issues between them despite having a free trade agreement (ANZCERTA) in place and despite the fact that the Trans-Tasman Mutual Recognition Arrangement (TTMRA) is recognized by both governments as a foundation for the trans-Tasman economic market.

After failed consultations with Australia regarding the measures imposed on the importation of New Zealand apples, New Zealand requested the establishment of a panel by the WTO's Dispute Settlement Body (DSB) on 6 December 2007, claiming that the measures imposed by Australia are scientifically unjustified under the WTO's Sanitary and Phytosanitary Measures (SPS) Agreement. On 21 January 2008, the DSB followed up on the request and set up the panel.

In August 2010, the panel report was circulated and confirmed and supports New Zealand's claims that Australia's measures are inconsistent with the WTO's SPS Agreement. Australia appealed the panel's decision; the case is currently under review by the Appellate Body. We provide more detail below.

This is the most recent development in the long-running dispute between Australia and New Zealand regarding the importation ban applied to New Zealand apples by Australia since 1921, based on the Australian Quarantine Act 1908 (AQA), the Australian Quarantine Proclamation 1998 (AQP),[9] and the application of phytosanitary measures recently specified in the final Import Risk Analysis report for apples from New Zealand of November 2006 (IRA).

Prior to 1921, New Zealand had market access to Australia for fresh apple fruit. The introduction and establishment of the fire blight disease in Auckland in 1919 led to an Australian ban on apple imports from New Zealand in 1921. New Zealand tried to have the ban lifted by applying for market access to the Australian fresh apple fruit market in 1986 and 1989. Both applications were rejected on the grounds of unresolved issues regarding the possibility of disease importation from fire blight affected orchards in New Zealand.

In 1995, with the support of a research study on fire blight and a pest list regarding New Zealand apples, New Zealand launched another application to regain market access. After an analysis by the Australian Quarantine Authority, the application was rejected in 1998. In early 1999, New Zealand submitted a new application, asking for a review of available risk-management options for New Zealand apples. The goal was to regain market access for New Zealand apples, relying on the provision in the SPS agreement requiring the "least trade restrictive" measure possible to satisfy legitimate concerns of the importing country. Since 1999, New Zealand has provided further research details in regard to pest and disease status in New Zealand.

Australia carried out an Import Risk Analysis in 2006, resulting in a recommendation that importation of New Zealand apples to Australia, except to Western Australia, be permitted subject to the following phytosanitary measures and stringent risk management conditions:

- Mandatory pre-clearance arrangements with Australian Quarantine and Inspection Service officers involved in all risk-management measures in New Zealand and auditing of the systems and processes used by New Zealand to certify exports.
- Orchard inspections undertaken for fire blight symptoms at an inspection intensity that would, at least to a 95 per cent confidence level, detect visual symptoms if shown by 1 per cent of the trees; this inspection should take place between 4 and 7 weeks after flowering when conditions for fire blight disease development are likely to be optimal. Orchards with any visual symptoms of fire blight disease would be disqualified from export.
- Use of disinfectant treatment (e.g. chlorine) in the packing house to prevent contamination of apples with fire blight bacteria.

- Inspection of all host trees in export orchards after leaf fall, during winter, for freedom from European canker disease. Orchards with any symptoms of European canker would be disqualified from export.
- Inspection in New Zealand of a random sample of 3,000 fruit from each lot for freedom from apple leaf curling midge. Detection of apple leaf curling midge would result in rejection of the lot or treatment. Alternatively, a treatment such as fumigation could be used for all export lots.
- Inspection for all other quarantine pests with remedial action taken (treatment or withdrawal of the lot) if any are detected.

The analysis concluded that no satisfactory risk management procedures could be identified for apple scab disease. Therefore, it proposed that imports of New Zealand apples into Western Australia not be permitted.

The proposed recommendations of the IRA were accepted by the Australian Government's Biosecurity Australia. The New Zealand Government, however, would not accept the measures proposed as representing the least trade restrictive measure possible to satisfy any scientifically justified concern. After unsuccessfully trying to solve the issue with the Australian Government bilaterally, the New Zealand Government initiated WTO dispute settlement procedures against Australia to resolve the long-standing dispute. In justification of this action, the New Zealand Government's Trade and Agriculture ministers stated that the "Final IRA imposed a very restrictive regime for [...] apple exports and requires measures that are not scientifically justified."[10] New Zealand's challenge to Australia's regime also cites the WTO's Japan decision where the WTO found import restrictions for fire blight to be unjustified for trade in commercial apples.[11] New Zealand especially criticized the import restriction for Western Australia, which claims to be free of apple scab (black spot) and considers New Zealand apples a risk factor.

Unfortunately, the New Zealand Government did not release any documents in regard to their claim that the measures imposed by Australia are scientifically unjustified: "To protect New Zealand's legal position in the WTO case, we cannot comment on that at this stage."[12]

Meanwhile, the WTO's director general convened its panel on 12 March 2008. Due to the nature and scope of the WTO dispute on New Zealand apples, including the panel's decision to seek the support of scientific and technical expert advice in regard to Article 11 SPS Agreement and Article 13 Dispute Settlement Understanding (DSU), the chairman of the panel informed the DSB on 19 September 2008 that the panel would be unable to issue its report within six months. The panel expected its final report to be issued to the parties by July 2009.[13]

In June 2009, the Chairman of the panel informed the DSB of a delay of the final report until January 2010. The panel report was finally concluded and circulated in August 2010, as noted earlier. It discusses the "16 phytosanitary measures adopted by Australia for the importation of New Zealand apples", including the relevant measures against the risk of fire blight. The panel report finds that Australia's measures are not based on proper risk management assessment and are inconsistent with the WTO's SPS Agreement (SPS) Article 5.1 and 5.2. Additionally the report finds the SPS measures adopted not being "based on scientific principles" according to Article 2.2 SPS and therefore, should "not be maintained without sufficient scientific evidence". Furthermore, the panel report established that the vast majority of the Australian measures are more restrictive to trade than necessary to achieve an appropriate level of SPS protection and are inconsistent with Article 5.6 SPS and that New Zealand's suggestion of the importation of "mature, symptomless apples" is an appropriate alternative to Australia's measures under Article 5.6 SPS as is "the inspection of a 600-unit sample from each import lot". As of 31 August 2010, the Panel report is under appeal as a result of Australia's decision to appeal to the Appellate Body, New Zealand followed on 13 September 2010.[14]

Standards and Conformance

The initial focus of cooperative efforts was on accreditation and quality assessment. An Agreement on Standards, Accreditation and Quality (ASAQ) in 1990 between the Australian federal and state governments and the New Zealand Government was followed in 1991 by the establishment of JAS-ANZ, a joint accreditation system, providing for a harmonized approach to auditing and certification of quality management systems on the basis of international standards.

A more far-reaching initiative was the agreement in 1995 to establish joint food standards. The relevant agreement, the Agreement on Establishing a System for Development of Joint Food Standards (the ANZFA agreement), provided for the establishment of a joint regulatory agency, the Australia New Zealand Food Authority (ANZFA), and a process leading to the finalization of a joint Australia New Zealand Food Standards Code by 1999. The arrangement on joint food standards is complemented by the Arrangement on Food Inspection Measures (AFIM) under which food products traded between the two countries other than those identified as "risk classified", will not be subject to any inspections beyond the domestic surveillance arrangements in each country.

Mutual Recognition

A more comprehensive approach to product standards is embodied in the Trans-Tasman Mutual Recognition Arrangement (TTMRA) signed in 1996, which covers occupational qualifications as well as product standards. The purpose of the TTMRA is to remove progressively regulatory barriers to the movement of goods and service providers between the two countries. In principle it means that a good which can legally be sold in one country can also be legally sold in the other, and a person registered to practise an occupation in one country is entitled to practise an equivalent occupation in the other.

The TTMRA is based on the pre-existing Mutual Recognition Agreement (MRA) between the federal, state, and territory governments of Australia, agreed in 1992, which in fact already contained an invitation to New Zealand to consider participation in a trans-Tasman mutual recognition scheme. Conceptually, therefore, the TTMRA extended the earlier MRA to include New Zealand.

Five goods sectors are subject to special exemptions under the TTMRA: therapeutics; hazardous substances, industrial chemicals, and dangerous goods; motor vehicles; gas appliances; and radio communication standards. In the case of three of these sectors, separate mutual recognition arrangements have subsequently been pursued. In the case of therapeutics, agreement was reached in 2003 to establish a joint agency for the regulation of therapeutic products, the Australia New Zealand Therapeutic Products Authority (ANZTPA). However legislation required to give effect to this agreement failed to pass the New Zealand Parliament. Work is being undertaken to address existing bilateral differences in the regulation of hazardous substances, industrial chemicals, and dangerous goods. In 2003 common regulatory requirements were introduced for nine radio communication product categories, leaving four product categories still covered by the special exemption because of historical differences in the frequency of radio bands used in the two countries.

One service sector, medical practitioners, is also subject to a special exemption from the TTMRA. There are, however, already mutual recognition-type arrangements in place covering doctors trained in Australia and New Zealand.

Trade in Services
One important strand of the implementation of the CER Trade in Services Agreement has been the gradual removal of sectors excluded under the inscriptions of each country. Currently only a few sectors, such as coastal shipping, remain covered by the inscriptions.

BOX 3
Trans-Tasman Mutual Recognition Agreement[15]

The *Trans-Tasman Mutual Recognition Arrangement (TTMRA)* is a 1996 non-treaty agreement between Australia and New Zealand, and is recognized by the governments of both countries as a foundation for the single trans-Tasman economic market. The agreement "applies to the movement of goods and people".[16]

The TTMRA is based on the Australian Mutual Recognition Agreement (MRA), agreed in 1992, as a response to the existing multiple regulatory environments across Australian states and territories. The MRA is based on two main principles:

(a) a good that may be legally sold in one state or territory may be sold in another state or territory, regardless of the differences in standards or other sale-related requirements between the states and/or territories; and

(b) a person registered to practise an occupation in one state or territory is entitled to practise an equivalent occupation in another state or territory, without the need to undergo further testing or examination.[17]

The MRA and the **TTMRA** require Australia and New Zealand to conduct five yearly **reviews** of the effectiveness of the mutual recognition schemes. The most recent review, by the Australian Productivity Commission, has just been concluded.

Reviews have also been commissioned for several specific issues, such as the impact on food regulations. In 2003, for example, Food Standards Australia New Zealand (FSANZ), the bi-national statutory authority in charge of developing common food standards to cover the whole food chain, recommended changes to the Australia New Zealand Food Standards Code (ANZFSC) as well as in the permanent exemption from the TTMRA of risk-categorized food.[18]

FSANZ found that, even though the process of harmonization of food regulations in the two countries was well advanced, differences still remained, imposing additional costs on the industry as well as having implications for public health and safety. It agreed that scrutiny and control are required of imports that pose a high or medium risk, and that the permanent exemption from the TTMRA for risk-categorized foods placed on lists of high-risk food imports is an appropriate form of protection for public health and safety. It also noted however that Australia and New Zealand have different lists, and that a harmonized list of high-risk food imports is necessary to facilitate further trade.

FSANZ recommended the creation of a permanent exemption in the TTMRA for all products not covered in the ANZFSC, with criteria to identify food related regulations that should not be subject to this exemption; and the abolition of the permanent exemption for risk categorized food commodities when the regulatory authorities have agreed to a joint high-risk food list.

The adoption of the review of food regulations is currently under way.

Further action was sometimes needed to tease out the operational details of how the agreement to liberalize services trade would be applied. In the case of media services, for example, a series of court actions focused on the issue of whether the CER agreement required that material produced in New Zealand be counted as "Australian content" for the purpose of Australian local content regulations.

The case of air services, one of the sectors excluded from the CER Agreement under the respective inscriptions of the two countries, was addressed by the conclusion in 1994 of arrangements for a Single Aviation Market (SAM). Lloyd (1995) describes how in the week before the single market was due to be implemented, the Australian Government announced that it would not permit Air New Zealand to operate domestic services in Australia. This triggered a chain of events that included a tortuous and ultimately disastrous takeover by Air New Zealand of the Australian airline Ansett as an alternative means of securing access to the Australian domestic market (Kissling 1998); the failure of Ansett, and near collapse of Air New Zealand, and its rescue by the New Zealand Government stepping in as majority shareholder.

The Single Aviation Market agreement was eventually implemented in 1996 and was subsequently reinforced by an Open Skies Agreement in 2000. The market for passenger air transport services between Australia and New Zealand has become very competitive, contested by several foreign airlines as well as Australian and New Zealand carriers. The Australian airline Qantas and now its subsidiary, Jetstar, operate an established network of domestic air services in New Zealand, but no New Zealand airline operates domestic services in Australia.

One evaluation of the ANZCERTA provisions on services can be found in Ochiai, Dee and Findlay (2009), which reviews the treatment of services in a number of agreements in the Asia Pacific region. Information was collected on the content of these agreements, across sectors and modes of supply, and converted into scores. Higher scores apply to more liberal agreements. ANZCERTA, along with the Australia-US FTA, emerges as relatively liberal, compared with the agreements signed by Japan or by Singapore. However the degree of difference between these agreements is not large. The largest differences occur in two important dimensions:

a)   The share of sectors excluded in CER is very low, estimated to be 8 per cent (based on the Central Product Classification (CPC) list of sectors), whereas other agreements, including ASEAN Free Trade Area (AFTA), have exclusion rates five times higher than that (the AFTA exclusion rate was estimated to be 90 per cent). Ochiai, Dee and Findlay also compare exclusion rates in services in free trade agreements compared with the exclusion rates in GATS of the same countries: again the ANZCERTA rate of exclusion is small compared with that in GATS commitments by Australia and New Zealand.

b) Provisions on services in trade agreements often list reservations or restrictions which apply (horizontally) to all sectors. Ochiai, Dee and Findlay list a significant number of horizontal reservations in agreements in the Asia Pacific. ANZCERTA has none listed.

Business Law

It was understood between the parties from the outset that the objective of business law harmonization would not be to establish identical Australian and New Zealand business laws, but rather to identify cases where differences in law increase the transaction and compliance costs faced by companies operating in both markets, and where those transaction and compliance costs could be reduced by harmonization.

Although a steering committee of officials was established to pursue and explore ways to give effect to the 1988 Memorandum of Understanding, progress was initially slow. Apart from the competition law initiatives implemented in parallel with the agreement to eliminate anti-dumping action, the main concrete result in the 1990s was a 1994 Memorandum of Understanding between the Australian Securities Commission and the Securities Commission of New Zealand.

A sense that progress needed to be accelerated led to the conclusion in 2000 of a Memorandum of Understanding on Business Law Coordination to supersede the 1998 MOU. A range of issues was singled out for early attention, including competition law, securities law, takeovers law, consumer protection law, electronic transaction law, disclosure regimes, cross-border insolvency, and patent examination.

Competition Policy

Over recent years the competition authorities of both countries, namely the Australian Competition and Consumer Commission (ACCC) and the New Zealand Commerce Commission (NZCC), have established an increasingly close relationship.[19] The deepening of this relationship has included regular staff exchange programmes, annual international cartel workshops, and ministerial council meetings (for example for consumer affairs) aimed at developing and improving networks and data-sharing platforms as well as the use of similar guidelines and cooperation in investigations, and coordination of enforcement where appropriate. Other areas of cooperation include technical assistance activities, exchange in expertise and resources, and coordination in investigations or enquiries of common interest (for example, merger reviews such as the one on the proposed Air New Zealand/Qantas merger).

In 2003 a work programme was agreed upon for coordination of competition policy issues, divided into short-term, medium-term, and long-term issues. Short-term issues include the appointment of Australian experts as lay members of the New Zealand High Court and encouraging the respective competition agencies to cooperate on leniency and merger procedures. Medium-term issues include developing legislation to enable information sharing between ACCC and NZCC and to explore opportunities for cross-appointments to the two agencies. A report on opportunities for greater convergence was commissioned by the Australian Productivity Commission (APC). This report appeared in 2004 as the Report on Australian and New Zealand Competition and Consumer Policy Regimes.

In regard to mergers, both countries prohibit those which have the purpose, the effect, or the likely effect of lessening competition. Any agreements, arrangements, or understandings between competitors are also proscribed. Nevertheless different assessments of regulatory errors (for example, the risk of approving a merger that turns out to be anti-competitive) can lead to different decisions. There are differences in attitudes to public benefits and in the welfare standards used to access "public" benefits. Furthermore, different appeal procedures and decision making authorities mean that complete business law harmony is far from being achieved.[20]

In cases where the parties are domiciled in different countries, the authorization process needs to take place in each one of these countries separately. Even though the same laws are applied to the same set of facts, different outcomes may be reached.[21]

Findlay and Round (2008) also observe that

> A somewhat unique feature of the Trade Practices Act in Australia and the Commerce Act in New Zealand is that both types of conduct can be administratively authorized (rendered immune from prosecution) if the parties can demonstrate ex-ante that any anti-competitive detriments arising from the conduct will be outweighed by any public benefits directly attributable to it. This process can be lengthy and cause significant commercial delays.[22]

Government Procurement

A review of Australia's National Procurement Agreement (NPA), to which New Zealand became a signatory in 1989, led to its

BOX 4
Trans-Tasman Dimensions of Competition Policy Issues Case Study: The Aviation Market

One of the best examples of trans-Tasman application of competition policy is the attempt by Air New Zealand and Qantas to set up a trans-Tasman agreement, and subsequent merger pressures.

The aviation market of Australia and New Zealand is regulated by the Open Skies Agreement (OSA). The OSA entered into force in 2000 and allows Australian and New Zealand international airlines to operate without any restrictions in both countries and beyond to third countries. By doing so it formalizes the 1996 Single Aviation Market agreement which allowed all Australian and New Zealand owned airlines to operate trans-Tasman and domestic services in both countries.[23]

Air New Zealand and Qantas Merger
The attempt by Air New Zealand and Qantas to set up a trans-Tasman agreement in which the two airlines proposed coordination of schedules and pricing for all flights within, originating from, and arriving into the two countries was denied by both competition authorities, the ACCC and NZCC. The rejection of the proposal was based on structural grounds — the likelihood of a combined trans-Tasman market share of 85–90 per cent, as Air New Zealand did not fly Australian domestic routes and appeared unlikely to do so in the future, and Qantas operated only limited domestic New Zealand services and appeared not to wish to expand these.

Following the decisions of both competition authorities, Qantas and Air New Zealand appealed these to the relevant bodies, namely the Australian Competition Tribunal, which granted the appeal, and the New Zealand High Court, which denied it. Thus, due to the necessity of approval in both jurisdictions the proposals were abandoned, at least temporarily.

In the meantime, as is to be expected in a highly dynamic market for passenger flights between Australia and New Zealand, competitive conditions had changed significantly. The entry of Virgin Blue, an Australian carrier, and Emirates, a large international carrier that used "dead" turnaround time to fly a return leg across the Tasman, offered much lower fares than those that had been offered previously by Qantas and Air New Zealand. Furthermore, Emirates offered true international class service. This resulted in a steep drop in market share for the two established trans-Tasman carriers, Air New Zealand and Qantas.

Following this development, the Australian tribunal found the structural approach unreasonable and applied a behavioural approach justified by the fact that there would only be limited prospect for future anti-competitive detriment from the conduct of the two airlines, such as raising their prices and restricting their schedules, due to the low cost and high standard of the new entrants, Virgin Blue and Emirates.

In April 2006, based on the findings of the tribunal, Qantas and Air New Zealand submitted a new trans-Tasman code-sharing alliance proposal (capacity and price control) to the ACCC. Due to the fact that the proposal contained no equity acquisition component, both airlines successfully bypassed the NZCC as in New Zealand intercountry agreements require only the approval of the minister for Transport, who had previously signalled support. Both airlines were confident that, even without the approval of the ACCC, the Tribunal would grant permission. Interestingly, after the ACCC issued a draft decision rejecting the new proposal, the airlines announced that they would not proceed with another appeal.

Source: Findlay and Round

After the proposed merger between Qantas and Air New Zealand was denied by the ACCC and the NZCC in 2005/06, several other merger talks have taken place. The pressures for consolidation continue, and thus the issues involved in the assessment of cross-border mergers will persist.

British Airways (BA) and Qantas held merger talks which ceased in December 2008, although a joint services agreement between BA and Qantas remains untouched, allowing both, with anti-trust immunity, to coordinate fares and capacity on the so-called Kangaroo route.

Qantas faces increasing competition on the US-Australia route, including via New Zealand.[24] Virgin Australia launched US flights in February 2009 and Delta Airlines, the world's largest airline since its merger with Northwest, began daily flights to Australia in July 2009. This means that Qantas now faces three non-stop Pacific rivals, rather than the single competitor, United Airlines, that it faced hitherto.

Meanwhile, Qantas is reported to be continuing a variety of merger talks (including with Malaysia Airlines), and AirAsia is reportedly a possible candidate for merger with the Qantas subsidiary JetStar.[25]

In general, the recent market changing developments in the trans-Tasman aviation market have resulted in downsizing after many years of growth, as the new competition has created overcapacity just as demand is falling. Recently, Virgin Blue and SkyAirWorld announced cuts in capacity and employment, Qantas has announced capacity reduction, and Skywest recorded a drop in passenger numbers and a resulting loss.

Virgin Blue further reported domestic fares at a seventeen year low, with yields impacted accordingly. Virgin Blue over the second half of 2009 also removed capacity from the domestic Australian market. Virgin Blue senior managers experienced pay cuts of up to 30 per cent.[26]

In February 2009, the Qantas group announced a decision to inject JetStar into the New Zealand domestic market, beginning in June 2009. The New Zealand domestic market was then serviced by Air New Zealand, Qantas, and Virgin Blue/Pacific Blue. JetStar would replace its parent Qantas as the third competitor. The entry of JetStar was likely to continue the "damage" that Virgin Blue had already done to Air New Zealand's domestic yields.[27] With Air New Zealand heavily reliant on the New Zealand domestic market, which accounted for more than 60 per cent of its customers, this move was interpreted as a strategy to reinforce pressure for merger talks between Air

New Zealand and Qantas, leading the two airlines to return to the ACCC and
NZCC.

According to International Business Times (2010), in September 2010, JetStar
announced that it would add an additional 39 daily flights into the domestic
New Zealand routes as of February 2011. With their move, JetStar group
chief executive Bruce Buchanan sees the airline to deliver almost 20 per
cent of domestic New Zealand flights.[28]

In general, the entry of Virgin Australia and Delta Airlines may be positive
movements for a possible future Qantas/Air New Zealand merger, as the
NZCC in particular might see the issues differently today.

renaming as the Australia New Zealand Government Procurement
Agreement (ANZGPA). In addition to the new name, the ANZGPA
extended the scope of the agreement somewhat beyond the
elimination of preferences by including commitments by the parties
to equality of treatment for each other's products and suppliers,
and to promote opportunities for each other's products and
suppliers to compete for government business on a value-for-
money basis.

Taxation Issues

The two governments successfully concluded a new Double
Taxation Treaty (DPT) in 1995 to replace earlier out of date DPTs.

The taxation issue that caused the greatest difficulty, however,
was the treatment of imputation credits in relation to dividends
received by one country's investors in the other country, following
the introduction of imputation credits in both countries. While
mutual recognition by the tax authorities in each country of
imputation credits received by their taxpayers from investments
in the other country might seem to be a natural extension of the

concept in the context of trans-Tasman economic integration, in practice the issue proved very intractable. Concern over erosion of tax bases was often cited as a key source of difficulty.

The non-recognition of imputation credits received in the other country has significant implications for trans-Tasman investment. It means that in effect there is a significant penalty attached to investing in the other country, compared with investing in the investor's home country.

Technology

Cooperation between Australia and New Zealand on technology issues has begun to emerge. The leading forestry research organizations in the two countries, Commonwealth Scientific and Industrial Research Organization (CSIRO) in Australia and SCION (formerly the Forest Research Institute), are pooling their knowledge and expertise in a joint venture known as Ensis, which aims to avoid duplication in research and to provide better and more timely technology outcomes for stakeholders. In biotechnology, the Australia-New Zealand Biotech Alliance (ANZBA) aims at joint promotion of the two countries' industries and capabilities in the biotechnology field.

Movement of People

Bilateral policy developments in relation to the movement of people have left in place the essential freedom of movement, but have sought to address consequential issues relating to entitlements to welfare benefits, state funded medical treatment, and pensions, and the associated cost implications for the two governments, as well as the Australian Government's requirement for enhanced control over movements of people in and out of Australia.

Earlier arrangements, whereby New Zealanders in Australia enjoyed immediate access to all Australian benefits, and vice versa for Australians in New Zealand, were viewed by Australia with increasing dissatisfaction, as migration from New Zealand to Australia increased substantially from the 1980s. By the end of the 1990s the initial counter-measures, involving stand-down periods prior to new arrivals being eligible for benefits in the other country and annual reimbursement payments by the New Zealand Government to the Australian Government, had come to be regarded by the Australian Government as seriously inadequate, and the issue had become a serious irritant in the bilateral relationship.

In 2001 the Australian Government introduced a requirement that subsequent new arrivals from New Zealand would have to qualify as permanent residents of Australia before being eligible for some Australian welfare benefits. In 2002 a new Social Security Agreement (SSA) was introduced between the two governments, whereby the costs of benefits paid to pensioners, veterans, and severely disabled people who have lived parts of their working lives in both countries would be shared between the two governments, with each government paying its share directly to the beneficiaries. Earlier, in 1998, a Reciprocal Healthcare Agreement had restored reciprocity in health care access available to citizens travelling between the two countries, while a child support agreement provides reciprocity in the enforcement of child support payments in the two countries.

The legal requirement introduced in Australia for all non-citizens in Australia to hold visas was accommodated in the case of New Zealand visitors by the introduction of a Special Category Visa (SCV). In practical terms no change was experienced by the New Zealand visitors, who continued to need only valid New

---

BOX 5
Trans-Tasman Movement of People

Under the Trans-Tasman Travel Arrangement (TTTA), citizens of Australia and New Zealand enjoy reciprocal access to enter, reside, and work in each of the two countries. The trans-Tasman freedom of movement is seen as a key in the relationship of Australia and New Zealand. Estimates vary between 389,000 and 521,200 for the number of New Zealand citizens living in Australia, and between 60,000 and 63,000 for Australian citizens living in New Zealand. As of 30 June 2008, the Australian Government's Department of Immigration and Citizenship gives the number of 521,200[29] New Zealand citizens residing in Australia compared with 470,000[30] citizens given by the Australian Government's Department for Foreign Affairs and Trade for November 2008, and 389,000[31] for December 2008 by The New Zealand Ministry of Foreign Affairs and Trade.

According to the government statistics, there are approximately two million short-term Trans-Tasman visits each year.

Free movement and the possibilities for citizens to work in each other's country have highlighted issues related to social security, health, and taxation. The TTTA has been supplemented by the Social Security Arrangement, the Reciprocal Health Arrangement, and the Child Support Agreement. The Double Taxation Agreement handles tax issues evolving as a result of ANZCERTA.

Historical Overview
A bilateral social security agreement between Australia and New Zealand had been in place since 1948, developing into a "full host country agreement" in 1969 under which all New Zealand citizens enjoyed full access to all Australian benefits, as did Australian citizens in New Zealand. The Trans-Tasman Travel Arrangement (TTTA) was formalized in 1973. This "Arrangement" consists essentially of a series of ministerial understandings, duly reflected in immigration procedures in each country, that allow

Australians and New Zealanders to visit, live, and work in each other's country without restriction.

The increasing immigration flows from New Zealand to Australia in the 1980s, and the implied financial burden for Australia, led the Australian Government to ask for new arrangements. These came into force in 1986 and 1994, for example, the introduction of so-called stand-down periods prior to new arrivals becoming eligible for Australian social security benefits and an annual reimbursement system between both countries under which New Zealand paid some NZ$165 million to Australia for coverage of old-age veterans', invalids' and single-parent benefits received by New Zealand citizens living in Australia. In 1999, Australia claimed that it was incurring total costs of social security benefits paid to New Zealand citizens amounting to nearly A$1 billion, whereas New Zealand responded that New Zealand citizens were paying some A$2.5 billion in taxes in Australia. The Social Security Agreement (SSA) was introduced as a way of resolving these issues between the two governments.

The Social Security Agreement (SSA) of 2002 gives Australians living in New Zealand and New Zealanders living in Australia (in possession of the special category visa), under certain circumstances, the option to claim pension funds and to access social security. It gives people who spent parts of their lives in both countries the right and the opportunity to claim financial support (such as age pension benefits if sixty-five years old or over, and have resided in Australia and New Zealand for a total of at least ten years). Under the agreement, the two countries share responsibility for paying pensions for the aged and disabled persons in this category.

The Reciprocal Healthcare Agreement of 1998 reaffirmed health care access for citizens of Australia travelling in New Zealand, and New Zealanders travelling in Australia, and thus restored reciprocity in the level of health care access available to visitors travelling between the two countries.

This means that Australians visiting New Zealand and vice versa will continue to have the same access as local residents to treatment in the public health system for general and emergency medical requirements.

> The Australia-New Zealand child support agreement ensures reciprocity in the enforcement of child support payments from parents living in Australia, who are financially liable for children in New Zealand, and vice versa. The issue arose due to an estimated 8,000+ New Zealanders who are financially liable for children in New Zealand but living in Australia. Only about one eighth of them pay child support. The agreement also covers the less common payments of spousal maintenance, which the New Zealand Inland Revenue agency estimates to involve about 600 people in New Zealand.
>
> The agreement allows the governments of Australia and New Zealand to supply each other with necessary details of liable parents' income and their addresses.
>
> The Double Taxation Agreement of 1995 contains provisions to avoid double taxation and the prevention of fiscal evasion in relation to income flowing between Australia and New Zealand. In February 2003, the agreement was extended to include certain companies resident in the other country. The reform addressed the "triangular tax" problem. Australian shareholders who invested through a company residing in the New Zealand, which then went on to earn income and pay taxes in Australia, found that they were unable to benefit from the imputation credits. The same was true for people from New Zealand. Therefore, since 2003, Australian shareholders of New Zealand companies have been able to access franking credits arising from the payment of Australian taxes by these companies, and vice versa.

Zealand passports in order to enter Australia. On entry they are deemed to have applied for visas and to have automatically received SCVs, which is recorded electronically. The date of arrival in Australia stamped on the passport is sufficient evidence that they are holders of SCVs.

7. Pursuit of a Single Economic Market (SEM)

For many years ANZCERTA was the only preferential trade agreement in which either country was involved, excluding the non-reciprocal South Pacific Regional Trade and Economic Cooperation Agreement (SPARTECA) with the independent Pacific island states, and Australia's Papua New Guinea-Australia Trade and Commercial Relations Agreement (PATCRA) with Papua New Guinea. From 2000 onward however, first New Zealand, and then Australia, became active participants in the rapid spread of preferential trade agreements in the Asia-Pacific region. Pursuit of economic integration with other partners in the Asia-Pacific region was being accorded an increased priority by both countries. These developments raised questions over the degree of priority that both countries would in future place on their bilateral relationship, especially as they chose to pursue their new preferential arrangements individually rather than jointly.

Rather than allow the bilateral economic relationship to wither, however, the two countries decided instead to try to rejuvenate it. An important step in this direction was the creation by the two governments of the Trans-Tasman Leadership Forum, comprised of business leaders and other experts and leading figures from both countries. The forum meets annually and is charged with identifying and prioritizing avenues for deepening the economic relationship. At the governmental level the decision to rejuvenate the relationship was encapsulated in the commitment by the two countries in 2004 to pursue the achievement of a Single Economic Market (SEM). This commitment has been followed by significant developments in a number of areas.

Rules of Origin

In 2006 the two countries agreed on a major change in the ANZCERTA rules of origin, involving a switch to Change in Tariff Classification (CTC) as the principal basis for determining origin, with exporters retaining the option of using the old RVC-based rules for a further five years. For some products, mainly in the textile and apparel area, a "dual" requirement was imposed whereby the RVC rule and a CTC rule had to be satisfied simultaneously, while for a very small number of products in one apparel sub-heading, the RVC rule was retained as the sole rule of origin. These provisions were intended to allay concerns of industries in both countries that had expresses serious reservations over the change to CTC rules. The change was implemented in 2007.

It is interesting that this policy change contradicted the recommendations of a review undertaken by the Australian Productivity Commission (APC) in 2004 (APC 2004, and Gali and Gretton 2005). The APC had recommended retention of the RVC-based rules, but with some modifications designed to make them considerably more trade facilitative, the most significant of the proposed modifications being that automatic duty-free entry should be provided for any goods manufactured within the two countries, for which the difference between Australian and New Zealand duty rates is equal to, or less than, five percentage points. Looking ahead, the APC recommended that in the near future the two governments should aim to eliminate the content threshold and to align remaining non-zero MFN rates in the two countries' tariff schedules so that goods from all sources could enter the two countries on a common basis. In effect the APC was proposing that ANZCERTA should adopt the key features of a customs union.

The switch to CTC rules has been reflected subsequently in the approach taken by both Australia and New Zealand in negotiations of FTAs with other countries. It also aligns the two countries with the approach taken by the United States and increasingly by other countries in the Asia-Pacific region.

BOX 6
ANZCERTA — Rules of Origin

RoO in general
By definition of the WTO, the "Rules of Origin (RoO) are the criteria needed to determine the national source of a product. Their importance is derived from the fact that duties and restrictions in several cases depend on the source of imports."[32]

RoO can be defined in different ways, such as the application of the criterion of change of tariff classification, the *ad valorem* percentage criterion, or the criterion of manufacturing or processing operation. Depending on how they are specified, RoO "can restrict trade, misdirect investments, inhibit productivity growth and reduce welfare" from levels attainable with other specifications.[33]

Additionally, firms face administrative costs of doing business, which includes complying with paperwork and other bureaucratic requirements, and the customs authorities face administrative and auditing costs due to the RoO.

In general, two main approaches are currently used to define the RoO.

First, the so-called current Regional Value Content (RVC) method where the "last process of manufacture" must be performed by "the manufacturer" in either of the member countries, and additionally not less than a certain percentage of the "factor cost" associated with that process must represent "qualifying expenditure", including material, labour and overheads.

Second, the so-called "change in tariff classification (CTC) model". "Under this method, substantial transformation is deemed to have occurred if the finished good has a tariff classification different from that of the inputs used in its production."[34]

RoO and ANZCERTA
Prior to 1 January 2007, the minimum requirements for claiming origin under the CER RoO were determined by the RVC and the so-called "50 per cent rule calculation" at the last process of manufacture. In other words,

"the last process of manufacture should have occurred in Australia or New Zealand, and at least one half of the factory or work costs of the goods should be made up from expenditure on materials, labour, or factory overheads originating in the area."[35]

Productivity Commission Report on RoO[36]

Dissatisfaction with the ANZCERTA RoO, mainly on the New Zealand side, had been a long-standing issue in ANZCERTA. By the early twenty-first century, both governments were ready to consider reform, recognizing the increasing importance and significance of the RoO and the difficulties some stakeholders faced due to their restrictive effect in some areas.

Accordingly, the Australian Productivity Commission (APC) was commissioned to undertake a "research project" to determine and analyse the general problems most stakeholders of ANZCERTA faced in regard to the RoO.

In its main finding, in its "Research Report on Rules of Origin under ANZCERTA", the APC points out that the RoO are discriminatory as they provide incentives for producers to purchase inputs from suppliers in Australia and/or New Zealand rather than from other, lower-cost countries. These additional costs can outweigh the benefits and gains from trade liberalization achieved by ANZCERTA.

The APC summarizes the general concerns raised by most stakeholders in regard to the RoO as follows:

- Restrictiveness of the "last place of manufacturing criteria" as it is not well suited to current production systems which tend to be more specialized and often rely on contracting-out and commission work
- Definition of manufacturing
- Difficulties in meeting the 50 per cent criteria. The necessary substitution of higher-cost and lower-quality local inputs to meet the 50 per cent rule reduces a firm's competitiveness.
- Uncertainty due to price of input material and general exchange rate volatility
- Compliance costs to meet the RoO

Furthermore, in its report, the APC discusses both the main methods of determining origin, and comes to the conclusion that the existing framework — the RVC method — should be retained, with the adoption of minor changes to reduce operational problems, combined with the liberalization of "the current rules by applying a waiver to provide duty-free entry for CER goods manufactured in Australia and New Zealand which face trans-Tasman tariff differences of 5 percentage points of less".[37]

The APC clearly states that the CTC model, even though proposed and favoured by a number of participants, differs significantly in detail. It considers that the adoption of the CTC method would result in only minor benefits for traders.

The APC notes the economic implications of the RoO in encouraging "trade diversion" away from least-cost sources, depending on three main factors:

- The margin between preferential tariff rates and MFN rates
  o In this regard the APC notes the significant MFN tariff reduction by both countries over the past twenty years, with the result that in 2002 the average margin of preference had been reduced to "a little over 3 per cent points for New Zealand exports to the Australian market; and less than 1 percentage point for Australian exports to the New Zealand market".[38]
- The overall stringency of the criteria for conferring origin.
- The extent to which restrictive RoO are used merely to limit benefits of preferential tariffs to members of an agreement.

The APC's recommendations as stated in its report are as follows:

1. The general RoO should remain unchanged, meaning a decision against the CTC model
2. Changes should be undertaken in the following areas:
   a. Replacement of the "last place of manufacturing" requirement with one based on "principal firm" as being defined as the one that performs or has performed the last process of manufacture in the ANZCERTA region.
   b. Adoption of the standard definition of manufacturing as contained in the Singapore-Australia Free Trade Agreement.

c. Underlining of the goal of a single economic market, a single set of rules implemented according to uniform practices to align the valuation and coverage of eligible costs in Australia and New Zealand.

d. As far as possible, the alignment and harmonization of legislation, regulations and customs guidance manuals in Australia and New Zealand.

3. The introduction of a "waiver", once granted not to be removed, to provide for automatic duty-free entry for any goods manufactured within the Australian-New Zealand region for which the difference between the Australian and New Zealand MFN tariff rates is equal to or less than 5 percentage points.

4. Before 2010, in order to further advance the goal of the ANZCERTA, the content threshold should be eliminated with only a "principal firm" manufacturing test to be applied, and the remaining non-zero MFN rates in the Australian and New Zealand tariff schedules should be aligned, with the goal of jurisdiction-neutral entry of merchandise from all sources on a common basis.

The last mentioned recommendation would have in essence established a customs union between the two countries.

The APC rejected the CTC method, pointing out that:

- The CTC model differs significantly from the RVC one, resulting in marginal net benefits for ANZCERTA trade partners and Customs agencies (for example rules for a particular product differs across CTC-based preferential trade agreements involving the same member).

- The CTC method does not treat industries or products uniformly — the extent of transformation involved in a change in tariff classification varies greatly between headings, resulting in inconsistent origin determinations across industry sectors. This could lead to trade distortion.

- A change to CTC adds to complexity and trade distortion because origin rules often differ between preferential trade agreements.

- There is a chance that the CTC method could be subject to manipulative practices due to limited transparency. Time consuming and costly negotiations with trading partners of ANZCERTA may be necessary.

- Secondary criteria involved in the implementation can add to protection levels and compliance costs.
- The CTC method and especially the classification are slow and inflexible in adapting to technological changes.

A supplementary report to the APC's "Research Report on Rules of Origin under ANZCERTA" — "The Restrictiveness of Rules of Origin in Preferential Trade Agreements" — points out that within the twenty different RoOs of different trade agreements analysed for restrictiveness, the ANZCERTA RVC method is one of the least restrictive, underlining the merit of the APC's suggestion to keep the RVC method in place.

Rules of Origin since 1 January 2007 [39]

Despite the critical view of the APC, the Governments of Australia and New Zealand adopted the CTC method, justifying it by pointing out that "the new approach reflects similar Rules adopted in Australia's recent free trade agreements with Thailand and the USA. It will simplify the administration of RoO and reduce compliance costs".[40] In the new rule (since 1 January 2007), a product will be covered by the ANZCERTA as long as the production or "manufacturing process in Australia of New Zealand involves a specified change in its classification under the global Harmonized Commodity Description and Coding System".[41] New product specific rules are introduced to determine the origin of goods, incorporating the change in tariff classification method. An appropriate change in the classification of a good thus becomes the evidence of "substantial transformation" of goods in production.

One objective of this change was to simplify the RoO's administration and thereby reduce the costs of compliance. However, the requirement for record keeping that existed prior to 1 January 2007 is only modified, not replaced. The new amendment still requires exporters (the principal manufacturer or producer) to maintain records relating to the origin of the products. As a new obligation, "among other things, records associated with the classification, origin or value of materials used to produce the goods" need to be maintained.[42]

For some products, mainly in the textiles and apparel area, a "dual" requirement was imposed whereby the RVC rule and a CTC rule had to be satisfied simultaneously. For a very small number of products in one apparel sub-heading the RVC rule was retained as the sole rule of origin.

For all other products a five-year transition period is provided in which the importers may claim origin either under the new CTC rule or under the previously used RVC rule.

The Governments of Australia and New Zealand agreed to review the new RoO after three years. Change to the new rules agreed at a review in August 2009 will result in considerable simplification of the CTC rules for some products, including the removal of some complex exceptions that had been written into the 2007 CTC rules, the removal of almost all "dual" RoO requirements, and the conversion by 2012 of all remaining RVC rules to CTC. These changes will come into effect after they have been ratified by the Parliaments of both countries. The five year transition period, during which exporters retain the option of using the previous RVC rules, is maintained. An RVC alternative to the CTC rules will continue to be available beyond 2012 for a very small number of products where an RVC rule is seen to be advantageous.

The so-called "wholly obtained goods" rule remains in place. These are goods that are obtained or produce entirely in Australia or New Zealand. These are, for example, mineral products, vegetables, or agricultural products, and live animals born and raised in the trans-Tasman countries.

Exceptions from the RoO are made for specific purposes, as long as they are not used "as a means of arbitrary or unjustified discrimination or as a disguised restriction on trade". These include:

- Protection of essential security interests
- Protection of public morals
- Protection and prevention of disorder or crime
- Protection of human, animal or plant life or health
- Protection of intellectual or industrial property rights
- Prevention of unfair, deceptive, or misleading practices
- The application of standards or of regulation for the classification, grading or marketing goods up

Experience with these subsequent Australian and New Zealand FTAs assisted in overcoming the concerns over CTC rules on the part of industries whose sensitivities had led to the inclusion of some relatively restrictive elements in the 2007 ANZCERTA rules. Reflecting this, changes to the new rules agreed at a review in August 2009 will result in considerable simplification of the CTC rules for some products, including the removal of some complex exceptions that had been written into the 2007 CTC rules, the removal of almost all "dual" RoO requirements, and the conversion by 2012 of all remaining RVC rules to CTC. These changes will align the ANZCERTA rules more closely with the RoO in the recently agreed ASEAN-Australia-New Zealand FTA (AANZFTA).

Business Law and Regulation

Work on aligning elements of the business law of the two countries has taken on new impetus since the commitment to SEM. This is especially the case in competition policy and law. In 2005, the Australian Productivity Commission (APC) recommended legislative reform to address barriers of cross-border agencies' co-operation.[43] Therefore, in August 2006, ACCC and NZCC signed a "Cooperation Protocol for Merger Review", which replaces the 1994 memorandum of understanding. The goal of the protocol is to reduce compliance costs for trans-Tasman businesses further, lower transaction costs for both agencies, and increase the effectiveness of the competition laws in both countries. The protocol is targeted at assisting the review of merger transactions by exchanging necessary information obtained from each of the two competitive agencies' merger review processes and functions. The protocol is, therefore, intended to improve the capacity of both agencies to deal with cross-border competition and consumer issues more effectively.[44] In 2007, a Cooperation Agreement was signed between the two authorities, focusing on boosting cooperation and consumer protection enforcement across the two countries.

A Treaty on Mutual Recognition of Securities Offerings was signed in 2006. Also in 2006, a review of the MOU on Business Law produced a revised agenda for the next five years. A Trans-Tasman Council for Banking Supervision has been established to enhance cooperation in banking regulation across the two countries, although significant differences remain between the two countries in their approach to banking regulation. A newly established Trans-Tasman Accounting and Auditing Standards Advisory Group has developed a protocol of cooperation between the two countries' accounting standards bodies.

The policy response in 2009 to the global financial crisis has thrown into sharp relief issues of banking supervision and regulation between the two countries. Australian-owned banks occupy an overwhelming share of the New Zealand banking market. This situation has developed over the years without apparent adverse consequences for the New Zealand economy or business sector, although the New Zealand Government did decide in 2001 to establish a state-owned bank, Kiwibank, with the express aim of applying greater competitive pressure to the major banks. New Zealand's Reserve Bank has also given consideration to how its approach to banking supervision should reflect the situation. The decision by both countries to support the banking sector in the two countries through government guarantees for deposits underlined the extent to which banking supervision and regulation in New Zealand must take account of the extent of Australian ownership of the sector. The New Zealand authorities had to design their own guarantee schemes carefully with reference to the guarantees being provided in Australia, with the aim of ensuring that risks and costs are appropriately shared between the two countries. Subsequently, after both governments have encouraged their banking sectors to assist their business sectors with accommodating treatment where possible, concerns have been raised in the New Zealand business sector that the Australian-owned banks are providing more favourable treatment to businesses in Australia than to businesses in New Zealand.

Taxation Issues

In 2008, following a meeting between finance ministers of the two countries, it was announced that Australia has agreed to move ahead with New Zealand on work towards introducing mutual recognition of imputation credits on dividends.

Investment

Commitment to the pursuit of the SEM has been accompanied by an undertaking to consider adding an investment component to ANZCERTA. In 2009 the two prime ministers made a commitment to the finalization of an Investment Protocol designed to lower regulatory barriers and compliance costs to businesses and thereby further promote investment between the two countries.

Border Controls

Also in 2009, the two prime ministers announced that exploratory work would be undertaken on the removal of border controls on movement of persons and freight between the two countries, so that these movements could in effect be treated as domestic movements.

8. Further Monetary Integration: A Monetary Union?

Given the degree of economic integration achieved between Australia and New Zealand, it is perhaps natural that the possibility of a monetary union between Australia and New Zealand should have been considered. Interest in this issue has been confined almost entirely to New Zealand. Little interest has been evident in Australia, perhaps because of the assumption that monetary union would necessarily involve the adoption by New Zealand of the Australian currency, and that the associated adjustment issues would be primarily a matter for consideration by New Zealand rather than Australia.

In New Zealand a substantial report on the issue was produced in 2000 (Grimes *et al.* 2000), and there have been a number of further publications dealing with the issue both by Grimes and by economists at New Zealand's Reserve Bank (see, for example, Grimes 2005, Bjorksten 2001, and Hunt 2005). This literature is reviewed by Lloyd and Song (2006). Essentially two possibilities have been under consideration: dollarization, whereby the New Zealand Government unilaterally adopts the Australian dollar as its currency, and a formal monetary government, whereby the two governments would jointly adopt a single currency with a single central bank and monetary policy. In the latter case it is typically assumed that the single currency would in practice be the Australian dollar and that the Australian central bank would assume the role of central bank for both countries.

In summarizing research on the issue, Lloyd and Song (2006) note that analysis has generally concluded that neither the benefits nor the costs of monetary union are likely to be large for New Zealand, although Grimes *et al.* (2000) did mount a case for the adoption by New Zealand of the Australian dollar as its currency (with the US dollar as a possible alternative). One Australian study of the issue, by Crosby and Otto (2002), concluded that monetary union is not in Australia's interest. Politicians have generally been cautious in discussing the issue, perhaps mindful of nationalistic sentiment in both countries. On the other hand,

Grimes *et al.* (2000) report the results of a survey of 400 New Zealand firms, showing a majority in favour of an irrevocable link to the Australian dollar. Hunt (2005) reports a nationwide poll showing 45 per cent in favour of an "Anzac dollar" (although there was less support for the adoption of the Australian dollar). Lloyd and Song (2006) note that there has been no discussion to date on the possible constitution of a common central bank in the event of a monetary union, and no discussion of measures to promote convergence of the two macroeconomies, the implication being that monetary union is not yet being considered as a serious possibility. They conclude that a case for monetary union has not yet been established.

9. The Economic Effects of ANZCERTA

This penultimate section of the report surveys the evidence from studies of the economic effects of ANZCERTA.

Approaches to Assessing FTA Effects

Most studies of the economic effects of ANZCERTA have focused on its impact on trade, typically the impact on merchandise trade, usually with a view to deriving estimates, or more commonly inferences, as to its impact on the overall economic welfare of the partners. As with all analyses of FTAs and other forms of preferential trade agreement, the analysis of the economic effects of ANZCERTA has typically focused on the relative strength of trade creation and trade diversion effects, as the first step towards reaching conclusions regarding overall welfare effects.

The removal of tariffs (and other trade barriers) on trade between the FTA members allows each member's goods to be sold in its partner's market at a lower price than previously. Some products that were uncompetitive in the partner market when they were subject to the partner country's tariff[45] will become competitive when that tariff is removed under the FTA, giving rise to increased intra-FTA trade in the form of imports by the partner country of these products that are newly competitive in its market.

The increased intra-FTA trade can be divided into three parts. One part simply involves the replacement of imports from previous foreign suppliers (who would remain the most competitive suppliers of imports if the tariff continued to be applied to products from all sources). This is trade diversion. A second part involves the replacement of less efficient domestic production in the partner by the more competitive imports from the other FTA member, while the third part reflects the increased overall purchasing by consumers in response to the lower prices. Trade creation is the combination of these latter two parts: it is the amount of increased intra-FTA trade that does not simply consist of trade diversion.

Trade creation (sometimes described, more precisely, as net trade creation[46]) yields a welfare gain to the importing member, the size of which depends both on the amount of trade created, and on the extent of the price fall in the domestic market of the importing member, brought about by the entry of duty-free imports from the partner. Trade diversion imposes a welfare loss, the size of which depends on both the amount of trade diverted and the difference between the duty-free prices of imports from inside and outside the FTA. In the simplest formulation, FTAs are considered to be welfare increasing if the welfare gains from trade creation exceed the welfare losses from trade diversion, and welfare reducing if the welfare losses from trade diversion exceed the welfare gains from trade creation.

The fact that welfare effects depend on price differences as well as changes in trade means that overall welfare effects cannot always be reliably estimated by simply comparing the amounts of trade created and diverted.[47] It is entirely possible for welfare to fall in an FTA where more trade is created (in the net sense) than diverted; this could occur if the extent of the price fall in the domestic market is small relative to the difference between the duty-free prices of imports from inside and outside the FTA. On the other hand it is true that an FTA cannot be welfare increasing if more trade is diverted than created.

There are other potential sources of gain or welfare loss that are omitted in the conventional analysis based on trade creation and trade diversion. In particular, no account is taken of possible terms-of-trade changes, which could be negative for one FTA partner and positive for the other. Economies of scale are often said to be important in FTAs, although Corden (1972) has shown that the existence of economies of scale, while introducing additional possible sources of welfare gain or loss, does not rule out the possibility of trade creation and trade diversion as sources of welfare gain or loss. Pro-competitive effects of FTAs are often highlighted as potential sources of welfare gains, but rarely quantified. The conventional analysis takes no account of adjustment costs either.

A further point highlighted specifically in relation to ANZCERTA in a 2004 report of Australia's Productivity Commission (APC) is the importance of pricing behaviour of firms within an FTA (APC 2004). The conventional analysis of FTAs typically assumes that firms within the FTA, where their cost structure allows them to do so, take advantage of the removal of tariffs on intra-FTA trade to sell their products in the partner market at a price below that of products from other foreign suppliers that remain subject to the partner's tariff.

APC (2004) points out however that it may be entirely plausible to suggest that Australian and New Zealand exporters "price up" to the tariff level in the ANZCERTA partner country.

To quote an example from APC (2004), suppose that manufacturers of jumpers are protected by MFN tariffs of 25 per cent and 19 per cent in Australia and New Zealand respectively. It may be assumed that New Zealand manufacturers set their prices in New Zealand to take full advantage of the 19 per cent New Zealand MFN tariff. When exporting to Australia they may choose to raise their prices further to take full advantage of the higher Australian MFN tariff, rather than undercutting existing suppliers to the Australian market by selling at a price comparable to their price in the New Zealand market. In this case there will be no change in the domestic market price of the importing partner, and ANZCERTA acts instead to provide an additional element of industry assistance to the New Zealand manufacturers. Applying this pricing assumption, APC (2004) calculated that in 2001–02 ANZCERTA increased "the average level of effective assistance to Australian and New Zealand manufacturing activities by 0.08 and 0.7 percentage points respectively, above that available without CER preferences" (APC 2004).

The APC study does not address the question of welfare effects. It is clear, however, that if the domestic price in the importing partner's market does not change, there can be no source of welfare gains for that partner. In a somewhat different context, Panagariya (1999) has shown that FTAs, where exporting firms are able to "price up" to the tariff-inclusive price in the partner market, are likely to be wholly trade diverting and therefore unambiguously welfare reducing. Whether the pricing behaviour of Australian and New Zealand exporters does in fact correspond to that assumed in the APC study is, of course, an empirical question, on which the APC provides no evidence.

The most widely used methodologies today for assessing the economic effects of FTAs are Computable General Equilibrium (CGE) simulations and gravity modelling. CGE modelling is a forward looking (*ex ante*) methodology that seeks to estimate the effects of future policy changes such as the establishment of FTAs. CGE simulations of FTAs produce estimates of changes in production, trade, and economic welfare. Since no CGE-based estimates of the effects of ANZCERTA are reported in this paper, this methodology will not be considered further here.

Gravity modelling is a backward looking (*ex post*) econometric methodology that seeks to identify and quantify the influence of the factors that explain past bilateral trade flows. The range of explanatory variables that can found in gravity models is very wide. Among those most commonly used are (for each pair of countries) the sum or product of the GDPs of each pair of countries, difference in per capita income, distance, the existence of a common border, a common language, common colonizer or common currency, real exchange rates, and whether one country in each pair is an island or landlocked. Estimates of the trade impact of PTAs are derived in gravity models through estimating coefficients on variables introduced into the models for this purpose, in the manner described below.

There are several recent gravity modelling studies that include estimates of the effects of ANZCERTA. In every case ANZCERTA appears as one of a large number of PTAs whose effects are being estimated. The principal purpose of these studies is typically to explore the trade effects of PTAs in general, rather than to evaluate the effects of individual PTAs such as ANZCERTA.

Another focus of interest in analysing the effects of an FTA such as ANZCERTA is the extent of the contribution of intra-industry trade (IIT) to the changes in trade following from the agreement. Intra-industry trade is thought to be associated with lower levels of adjustment cost than interindustry trade, because the adjustments brought about by intra-industry trade typically involves the shifting of resources within industries and within firms, rather than between industries. Two studies of the role of intra-industry trade in ANZCERTA will be briefly reviewed here.

An Early Assessment by Australia's Bureau of Industry Economics (BIE)

Before turning to the findings of the more recent gravity model studies on trade creation and trade diversion, the findings of an earlier study by BIE (1989), focused on the initial years of ANZCERTA, will be briefly summarized, along with estimates of the welfare effects of ANZCERTA.

The BIE produced estimates of trade creation and trade diversion under ANZCERTA from the perspective of Australia, using the somewhat simplistic method of Truman (1969), which is based on changes in the shares of domestic consumption attributed to domestic (Australian in this case) producers, exporters from the partner country (New Zealand in this case), and exporters from the rest of the world (RoW). A decrease in the domestic share is taken as an indication of gross trade creation,[48] reflecting the replacement of less efficient domestic production by more efficient imports. An increase in the partner share indicates intra-FTA trade creation, which may be offset by a decrease in the RoW share, indicating trade diversion, or, as in this case, complemented by an increase in the RoW share, indicating extra-area trade creation.

The BIE estimates cover a period beginning just before the launch of ANZCERTA, in 1981–82, and ending in 1986–87, just before the first major review. Industries are classified as "unaffected", meaning that their products were already duty-free at the onset of ANZCERTA, "affected", meaning that they were liberalized in accordance with the general timetable set out in ANZCERTA, and "modified", meaning that they were subject to slower liberalization under ANZCERTA. As noted earlier, the proportions of trans-Tasman trade in manufactures covered by these three categories were approximately 50 per cent, 6 per cent, and 44 per cent, respectively.

The trade creation and trade diversion ratios for Australia reported in the BIE study are presented in Table 2. Gross trade creation is found for each industry group, that is, the share of domestic Australian industry in consumption declined. The corresponding increase in the import share of consumption was positive for each group for imports both from New Zealand and the rest of the world, indicating that both intra-FTA and extra-area trade creation occurred. The BIE comments that the trade creating effects of simultaneous liberalization with the rest of the world appears to have outweighed any tendency to trade diversion arising from ANZCERTA. This is particularly evident in the increase in import shares for the "unaffected" industries. The fact that the

TABLE 2
Trade Creation and Trade Diversion Ratios: Changes in Shares
of Australian Domestic Consumption 1981–82 to 1986–87
(percentage points)

| | Industry Category Affected | | |
	Unaffected	Affected	Modified
Imports from NZ	+0.4	+0.2	+0.2
Imports from RoW	+3.7	+6.0	+1.6
Australian Industry	–4.1	–6.2	–1.8

Source: BIE (1989)

increase in share of New Zealand imports was much smaller than the increase in share of imports from the rest of the world also reflects in part the very small share of New Zealand in Australia's import trade. The largest increase in import share occurred in the "affected" industries, while at the other end of the scale there was little trade creation in the "modified" industries.

Lack of suitable data availability prevented the BIE from calculating corresponding trade creation ratios for New Zealand. The BIE observes, however, that it is likely ANZCERTA had a much greater trade creating effect in New Zealand, given the much greater penetration of the New Zealand market by Australian exports.

The BIE (1989) also used 1982–83 data to produce forward looking estimates of the potential welfare gains from ANZCERTA, on completion of the liberalization of merchandise trade under the agreement. Their methodology takes account of both traditional inter-industry specialization and intra-industry specialization where welfare gains can arise from both trade creation and cost reductions achieved through the exploitation of economies of scale. Their results indicate total potential welfare gains equal to about 22 per cent of the additional trade in manufactured goods created under ANZCERTA, with the gains to Australia and New Zealand equating respectively to 7.9 per cent and 13.7 per cent of the additional trade. On a per capita basis New Zealand's gains are eight times those of Australia. New Zealand's gains come overwhelmingly from trade creation, accounting for 93 per cent of the total gains for New Zealand, whereas only 32 per cent of Australia's gains are attributable to trade creation, with 68 per cent of the gains arising from cost reduction. This implies that gains for New Zealand derive predominantly from the ability to specialize and import cheaper

Australian products, while more of Australia's industries are able to remain competitive in the enlarged trans-Tasman market by exploiting economies of scale.

Gravity Model Estimates of Trade Creation and Trade Diversion

Gravity models have become very widely used to estimate the determinants of bilateral trade flows. As noted earlier the typical gravity model equation relates bilateral trade flows to a wide range of possible explanatory factors. The most common approach to estimating the effects on bilateral trade flows of preferential trading arrangements (PTAs), such as FTAs, has been to introduce two dummy variables for each PTA.

The first dummy variable takes a value of 1 when the two countries on either side of the bilateral flow are both members of the PTA in question, and zero otherwise. The coefficient on this dummy is taken as an estimate of how trade between the members of the PTA in question differs from the trade between a random pair of countries with otherwise similar characteristics. A positive (and significant) coefficient on the dummy is interpreted as indicating trade creation, meaning that the PTA has led to increased trade between its members.

The second dummy variable takes a value of 1 when one of the pair of countries in a bilateral trade flow is a member of the PTA in question while the other is not, and zero otherwise. Again, the coefficient on this dummy is taken as indicating how trade between pairs of countries, where one country is a member of the PTA in question and the other is not, differs from the trade between a random pair of countries with otherwise similar characteristics. A negative (and significant) coefficient on the dummy is interpreted as indicating trade diversion, meaning that the PTA has led to reduced trade between its members and countries outside the agreement. A positive coefficient is taken as indicating that the PTA has led to increased trade with non-members.

The sum of the significant coefficients on the two dummies is taken as an indication of the overall trade creating or trade diverting effect of the PTA. If the sum is positive, for example with a positive coefficient on the first dummy outweighing a negative coefficient on the second, this is taken as evidence of overall trade creation, with trade creation exceeding trade diversion. This would be the case also if both coefficients are positive. If the sum of the significant coefficients is negative, with a negative coefficient on the second dummy outweighing the positive coefficient on the first, or with both coefficients being negative, this is taken as evidence of an overall trade diverting effect of the PTA in question, with trade diversion exceeding trade creation.

Table 3 gives results for the two dummy coefficients for ANZCERTA in five gravity model studies that include ANZCERTA within their sample of FTAs.

These studies vary in method, range of explanatory variables, number of PTAs included, trade coverage, and periods covered. Also, some of the results are not statistically significant. Nevertheless a reasonably clear pattern is evident in the significant results, and for the most part, the results that are not significant conform to this pattern also. In all the significant results, the coefficient on the first dummy is positive, indicating that ANZCERTA has stimulated increased intrabloc trade, while the coefficient on the second dummy is negative, indicating a trade diversionary effect. In all cases the sum of the coefficients is positive, indicating that the trade creation effects outweigh the

TABLE 3
Results for ANZCERTA from Gravity Model Studies
using the "two dummies" approach
Estimates of Coefficients on each dummy

Study	Period Covered	Estimated Coefficients	
		1st Dummy ("Trade Creation")	2nd Dummy ("Trade Diversion")
Frankel (1997)	1970–92	1.554***	0.021
Li (2000)	1970–92	1.872***	–0.090
Gilbert, Scollay,	1984–98 (merchandise)	0.81***	–0.50***
Bora (2004)	1984–98 (manufactures)	0.90***	–0.62***
	1984–98 (agriculture)	0.69***	0.68***
	1997 (services)	–0.45	–0.35***
Lee and Park (2005)	1955–97 (random effects)	0.544	0.537
	1955–97 (fixed effects)	0.294	0.244
Tang (2005)	1989–2000 (pooled)	1.115**	–0.119**
	1989–92	0.458	–0.238**
	1993–96	1.194**	–0.167*
	1997–2000	0.931**	–0.199*

Source: Author's compilation from various studies

trade diversion effects, so that ANZCERTA can be regarded as a trade creating FTA.

This picture is, however, forcefully challenged by a study carried out at the Australian Productivity Commission by Adams *et al.* (2003), who are sharply critical of a number of earlier studies using gravity models to estimate the effects of PTAs, and introduced a number of additional features into their model to address the perceived shortcomings. These features and, where relevant, the shortcomings they are designed to address, may be briefly summarized as follows:

- Following Soloaga and Winters (2001) the second dummy in the conventional "two dummy" approach is replaced by two dummies intended to capture separately the effect of the PTA on the import and export trade of PTA members. The reason for doing this is that effects on imports and exports could be different. One of these "new" dummies takes a value of 1 when a member of a PTA is importing from another country, and is taken as an indicator of the effect of the PTA on the import trade of the PTA member and its trading partner. The other "new" dummy takes a value of 1 when a member of a PTA is exporting to another country, and is taken as an indicator of the effect of the PTA on the export trade of the PTA member and its trading partner. Positive coefficients on these two dummies are taken as indicators of extra-PTA trade creation, in one case by increasing imports from non-members, and in the other, by increasing exports to non-members. Negative coefficients indicate extra-PTA trade diversion, by diverting imports or exports away from non-members. As in the more traditional approach, another dummy is also used to indicate the effect of the PTA on trade between members of the PTA, taking a value of 1 when both countries are members of the given PTA, and zero otherwise; a positive coefficient on this dummy is regarded as indicating intra-PTA trade creation.[49] As in the "two dummy" case, the sum of the significant coefficients is taken to indicate whether the overall impact of the PTA is trade creating or trade diverting, with a positive sum indicating overall net trade creation, and a negative sum indicating overall net trade diversion.
- The PTA sample used by Adams *et al.*, containing eighteen PTAs, is much larger than in a number of other studies.
- The gravity equation specified by Adams *et al.* allows for

trade in both differentiated and homogenous goods, so that in principle the explanation of trade flows includes both intra-industry and interindustry trade.

- Earlier studies do not take account of differences between PTAs in the degree of liberalization that they embody. PTAs with limited and far-reaching liberalization provisions are treated equally. Adams *et al.* allow for differences in degree of liberalization by replacing the binary dummy conventionally used to capture the effect on intra-PTA trade with a Member Liberalization Index (MLI), the value of which reflects the degree of liberalization each PTA has embodied in its provisions. For each PTA the MLI takes a value of between zero and 1, with higher values of the index indicating more far-reaching liberalization. The MLI is further split into two sub-indexes: a merchandise MLI, aimed at capturing provisions related specifically to trade in agricultural and manufactured products, and a non-merchandise MLI, aimed at capturing provisions with a broader effect on all trade and investment flows, described by Adams *et al.* as "new age provisions". These include provisions on services trade, national treatment, investment, competition policy, government procurement, intellectual property, and movement of people. The coefficient on the non-merchandise MLI is estimated for all PTAs in the sample as a whole, while coefficients are estimated on the merchandise MLI for each individual PTA.

- In many earlier studies the zero or one values for the dummy variables are applied to all PTAs in the sample for the entire sample period, even though individual PTAs may have been in operation for only part (sometimes only a small part) of the period. Adams *et al.* take a "dynamic" approach in which their MLI takes a positive value only for years in which the PTA in question was actually in operation, and takes a value of zero for all other years. They contrast this with the "anti-monde" approach in which positive or zero values are assigned for all years in the sample, irrespective of when particular PTAs commenced operation. They produce estimates using both the "dynamic" and "anti-monde" approaches for comparison purposes.

- The traditional PTA-specific dummy variables do not take account of the size of the tariff preferences created by the PTA. A bilateral tariff variable may be introduced to control for this. As a check on the significance of this issue, Adams *et al.* perform estimates both with and without the bilateral tariff variable included.

- Many earlier studies, using cross-section analysis, are unable to control for variations in unobservable or non-measurable country specific or time specific factors that may influence bilateral trade. Inability to control for these factors is likely to result in upward bias in the estimates of the coefficients of the PTA-specific dummy variables. The use of panel data allows Adams *et al.* to control for these effects. They choose for this purpose a fixed-effects approach in preference to the alternative random-effects approach, on the grounds that the requirement of the latter, for the unobserved effects to be uncorrelated with the included explanatory variables, is unlikely to be satisfied. The gravity equation of Adams *et al.* is thus estimated in Tobit form with fixed effects. For comparison purposes they also undertake estimates without fixed effects.

- There is zero bilateral trade between many pairs of countries in the world. Excluding these observations, as is done in many studies, will tend to give exaggerated weight to the positive bilateral trade flows. Adams *et al.* include values for trade in all bilateral links between the countries in their sample, regardless of whether the trade is positive or zero in each case. The relevant dependent variables are thus censored and a Tobit estimation procedure is used to take account of this. The resulting truncation of the distribution of the error terms is also taken into account.

• Adams *et al.* report marginal effects as well as the raw maximum likelihood Tobit effects. For technical reasons they use the marginal effects in assessing the trade creating or trade diverting properties of each PTA. They also note however that while the two types of effects differ, in qualitative terms they deliver the same results.

The additional features introduced by Adams *et al.* add up to a very considerable development of the gravity model methodology as used for assessing the effects of PTAs. The significance of this development is that their results show a dramatic difference from the results of earlier (and some later) studies. Whereas earlier studies have generally led to the conclusion that most PTAs deliver net trade creation, Adams *et al.* find that most PTAs in their sample are net trade diverting, including in particular major and/or more comprehensive PTAs such as NAFTA, the European Union/European Community, MERCOSUR, and ANZCERTA.[50] Their study therefore represents a very substantial challenge to the conventional wisdom regarding the trade effects of PTAs, as assessed by the gravity model methodology.

For the purpose of this report, the key finding is that ANZCERTA is included in the PTAs found to be trade diverting, in contrast to the findings of most earlier studies. Table 4 summarizes the estimates of Adams *et al.* of the PTA-specific dummy

TABLE 4
Gravity Model Results for Trade Effects of ANZCERTA
(Adams *et al.* 2003)

Period: 1970–97
Tobit Maximum Likelihood Estimates except where indicated

	Dummy 1 (Intra-PTA Trade)	Dummy 2 (Import Diversion)	Dummy 3 (Export Diversion)	Net Effect: Trade Creation (TC) or Trade Diversion (TD)
Dynamic PTA Indexes				
w/o fixed effects	–28.851***	3.329***	8.040***	TD
with fixed effects	–24.243***	–2.226***	–2.073***	TD
with fixed effects (marginal effects)	–18.639	–1.710	–1.591	TD
Anti-monde PTA Indexes				
w/o fixed effects	–16.504***	2.285***	7.650***	TD
with fixed effects	–17.251			–

Source: Author's compilation from various studies.

coefficients for ANZCERTA. The results are somewhat remarkable. The estimates of the coefficients on the dummy assigned to intra-PTA trade is strongly negative, and is also significant in all of the raw maximum likelihood estimates, while the coefficients on the "import diversion" and "export diversion" dummies are positive and significant when fixed effects are not included. Adams *et al.* note that exclusion of fixed effects is likely to give rise to an upward bias in estimates of the coefficients on the PTA-specific dummies. When fixed effects are included in the dynamic version, the coefficients are negative and significant for all three dummies, suggesting that ANZCERTA not only gives rise to lower trade between the two members, but also generates trade diversionary falls in both the imports and exports of the members.

This is an outcome that occurs with only three other PTAs in the Adams *et al.* sample: the European Union/European Community, the EU-Poland FTA, and the somewhat dubious case of PATCRA. The more usual outcome in the Adams *et al.* results, and also an outcome more consistent with standard formulations of the effects of PTAs, is a positive coefficient on the intra PTA trade dummy and negative coefficients on the other two dummies. Furthermore, unlike a number of other PTAs in the Adams *et al.* sample, the estimates for ANZCERTA show it to be trade diverting when the PTA dummies are defined in anti-monde form as well as when they are defined in dynamic form.

Adams *et al.* do caution that "in agreements with a small number of members, the intra-PTA trade effect is estimated imprecisely, with a large standard error, while the extra-PTA effect can be estimated more accurately. Thus, the findings for those PTAs, such as (ANZCERTA), with a small number of members are less robust than those for larger PTAs".

Beyond this, Adams *et al.* offer some tentative explanations for the finding of trade diversion for ANZCERTA and some other prominent PTAs, not all of them convincing. They suggest, for example, that rules of origin cause the amount of trade generated by an FTA to fall short of its potential. While this is certainly true, it is less obvious that this effect would be strong enough to produce a negative coefficient on the intra-PTA trade dummy (although it should be noted, as Adams *et al.* explain, that the PTA dummies do not test for absolute changes in the trade patterns of members, but for whether these changes in trade have been larger or smaller than the average changes across the entire sample of countries). As another possibility, they suggest that the control variable "may not capture fully the way that reductions in transport costs have raised the attractiveness of extra-bloc as opposed to intra-bloc trade for CER members over time".

Perhaps the most intriguing of their tentative explanations concerns the large amount of unilateral non-discriminatory liberalization in the world economy during the sample period. The resulting boost in trade, in absolute terms, with both members and non-members, may have raised the "benchmark of normal trade" against which the PTAs have been assessed. If trade between ANZCERTA members did not keep pace with the lifting of the "benchmark", a negative impact on intra-PTA trade could be recorded. This still leaves open the question of why this should have been the case.

DeRosa (2007) sets out to challenge the robustness of the finding of Adams et al. that most PTAs (at least in their sample) are trade diverting. He employs a larger dataset, containing 159 countries as against 116 countries in the datasheets of Adams *et al.*, and a different model, both taken from Rose (2004).[51] The "core" explanatory variables specified in the Rose model are similar to those found in Adams *et al.*, except that Rose's dataset does not include observations on tariffs and exchange rates. DeRosa also covers a slightly longer sample period (1970–99) than Adams *et al.* (1970–97).

A number of the features of the model used by Adams *et al.* are incorporated by DeRosa, such as the fixed effects variables and PTA-specific indicator variables, the latter specified in "dynamic form" and weighted by MLI values as in Adams *et al.*, using the same MLI values. In addition to performing an analysis on the same sample of PTAs as Adams *et al.* DeRosa also conducts a separate analysis on a much larger sample of forty-six PTAs.[52]

In addition to estimations using the Tobit regression framework with fixed effects employed by Adams *et al.*, DeRosa also experiments with the following additional frameworks:

- Ordinary Least Squares (OLS) and fixed effects with truncated data[53]
- OLS and fixed effects with censored data[54]
- Random Effects (RE) with both truncated and censored data
- Tobit random effects regression model

When using the random effects approach DeRosa departs from Adams *et al.* in specifying the country fixed effects on a country pair basis. In the case of random effects with truncated data for the sample of forty-six PTAs, DeRosa compares the results from using the three dummies of Soloaga and Winters (2001) with those from using a "two dummy" approach by Rieder (2006), where one dummy is designed as usual to capture inter-PTA trade effects, and the second dummy is specified to capture trade diversion effects represented by the change in imports from non-member countries only.

Results for the various estimations are reported for both total merchandise trade and total manufacturing trade. By utilizing all these variations DeRosa provides sixteen separate estimates of the coefficients on the three PTA-specific dummy variable for the PTAs in the Adams *et al.* sample, and eighteen separate estimates of these coefficients for the PTAs in the sample of forty-six PTAs.

In general DeRosa's experiments yield mixed results in relation to the trade creating and trade diverting properties of PTAs in the two samples. While a significant number of PTAs are assessed as trade diverting, most of the procedures used by DeRosa produce findings of net trade creation for the majority of the PTAs in either sample, in contrast to the finding of Adams *et al.* that the overwhelming majority of PTAs in their sample are trade diverting. DeRosa thus does appear to have cast doubt on that finding, even though he may not have succeeded in fully restoring the conventional wisdom that the vast majority of PTAs are likely to be trade creating. In particular, most of the larger PTAs, such as NAFTA, the European Union, MERCOSUR and AFTA, which were found to be trade diverting by Adams *et al.*, appear almost invariably as trade creating in DeRosa's results. In this light it is particularly striking that ANZCERTA continues to show as a trade diverting PTA in a significant proportion of DeRosa's results.

The results from DeRosa for ANZCERTA for total merchandise trade are shown in Table 5. ANZCERTA shows as a trade diverting PTA for the Adams *et al.* sample in the OLS estimates, and for the sample of forty-six PTAs in the truncated OLS estimates without country effects, and the truncated RE estimates with country effects. The coefficients on the first dummy, capturing the intra-PTA trade effects, are invariably positive, although several of them are not significant, and it is significant coefficients on the third dummy variable, and sometimes the second and third dummies together, that are responsible for the findings of net trade diversion.

The results for ANZCERTA's total trade in manufactured goods are shown in Table 6 for the Adams *et al.* sample and in Table 7 for the sample of forty-six FTAs. The results for the Adams et al. sample are especially striking, with ANZCERTA being assessed as trade diverting in all but one case. It is noticeable that none of the coefficients on the first dummy, some of which are negative and some positive, are significant, while the coefficients on the third

TABLE 5
Gravity Model Results for Trade Effects of ANZCERTA
(DeRosa 2007)

Total Merchandise Trade 1970–99

	Dummy 1 (Intra-PTA Trade)	Dummy 2 (Import Diversion)	Dummy 3 (Export Diversion)	Net Effect: Trade Creation (TC) or Trade Diversion (TD)
Sample:				
Adams *et al.*				
Truncated (OLS)				
w/o country effects	0.44	–0.95***	–1.53	TD
with country effects	0.41	0.41**	–0.90***	TD
Truncated (RE)				
w/o country effects	1.75*	0.19	–1.22***	TC
with country effects	1.79*	0.21	–1.24***	TC
Sample:				
46 PTAs				
Truncated OLS				
w/o country effects	0.42	–0.32***	–0.28*	TD
with country effects	0.28	0.30***	–0.22***	TC
Truncated (RE)				
w/o country effects	0.61*	0.18***	–0.31***	TC
with country effects	0.63**	0.24***	–0.31***	TD
Truncated (RE):				
Rieder Indicators				
w/o country effects	0.60*	0.21***		TC
with country effects	0.21***	0.25***		TC

Source: Author's compilation from various studies.

TABLE 6
Gravity Model Results for Trade Effects of ANZCERTA (DeRosa 2007)

Total Manufacturing Trade 1970–1999
PTA Sample: As per Adams et al. (2003)

	Dummy 1 (Intra-PTA Trade)	Dummy 2 (Import Diversion)	Dummy 3 (Export Diversion)	Net Effect: Trade Creation (TC) or Trade Diversion (TD)
OLS and Tobit				
Truncated (OLS)				
w/o country effects	–0.45	–0.29	–0.42	TD
with country effects	–0.74	1.52***	–1.15***	TC
Censored (OLS)				
w/o country effects	0.64	–1.46***	–0.05	TD
with country effects	nc	nc	nc	TD
Censored (Tobit)				
w/o country effects	–0.04	–2.01***	–0.90***	TD
with country effects	0.39	0.40	–1.31***	TD
Random Effects				
Truncated (RE)				
w/o country effects	–0.74	0.82***	–1.45***	TD
with country effects	–0.56	0.96***	–1.57***	TD
Censored (RE)				
w/o country effects	0.48	0.16	–1.34***	TD
with country effects	0.64	0.20	–1.52***	TD
Censored (RE Tobit)				
w/o country effects	0.98	–0.02	–1.54***	TD
with country effects	0.95	0.03	–1.71***	TD

Source: Author's compilation from various studies.

TABLE 7
Gravity Model Results for Trade Effects of ANZCERTA (DeRosa 2007)

Total Manufacturing Trade 1970–99
PTA Sample: Sample of 46 PTAs (DeRosa 2007)

	Dummy 1 (Intra-PTA Trade)	Dummy 2 (Import Diversion)	Dummy 3 (Export Diversion)	Net Effect: Trade Creation (TC) or Trade Diversion (TD)
OLS and Tobit				
Truncated (OLS)				
w/o country effects	0.33	–0.37**	0.38**	TC
with country effects	–0.07	0.73***	–0.30**	TC
Censored (OLS)				
w/o country effects	0.80**	–0.96***	0.64***	TC
with country effects	0.57*	0.31***	–0.22***	TC
Censored (Tobit)				
w/o country effects	0.54	–1.26***	1.04***	TD
with country effects	0.34	0.31***	–0.27***	TC
Random Effects				
Truncated (RE)				
w/o country effects	–0.46	0.44***	–0.35***	TC
with country effects	–0.40	0.55***	–0.40***	TC
Truncated (RE): Rieder Indicators				
w/o country effects	–0.26	–0.05		–
with country effects	0.57***	0.70		TC
Censored (RE)				
w/o country effects	–0.03	0.16***	–0.23***	TD
with country effects	0.04	0.23***	–0.30***	TD
Censored (RE Tobit)				
w/o country effects	0.04	0.14**	–0.33***	TD
with country effects	0.07	0.21***	–0.39***	TD

Source: Author's compilation from various studies.

dummy are invariably negative, and all but one of them is significant. The coefficients on the second dummy are generally positive in the random effects estimates, although few of those coefficients are significant. The coefficients on the second dummy are all negative in the OLS and Tobit estimates without country effects, and the two largest of those are significant. Inclusion of country effects in the OLS and Tobit estimates produces two positive coefficients, the larger of which is significant.

The pattern of estimated coefficients is quite similar for the sample of forty-six PTAs. The coefficients on the third dummy variable are always significant and are negative for all the random effects estimates, and for all the OLS and Tobit estimates where country effects are included. They are positive, however, when country effects are omitted from the OLS and Tobit estimates. There is a mixture of positive and negative coefficients on the first dummy, but the only significant ones are two positive coefficients in the OLS estimates with censored data, and a positive coefficient in the random effects estimate with country effects using the Rieder indicators. The coefficients on the second dummy are positive in all but one of the random effects estimates, and all but one of these positive coefficients are significant. As was the case with the Adams *et al.* sample in the OLS and Tobit estimates the coefficients on the second dummy are all negative and significant when country effects are omitted, but this time all the coefficients become positive and significant when the country effects are included.

The results for the sample of forty-six PTAs differ from those for the Adams *et al.* sample in the greater incidence of net trade creating effects, which are found in somewhat more cases than net trade diverting effects.

The evidence from DeRosa's results on whether ANZCERTA is a trade creating or trade diverting PTA is thus equivocal, to say the least. While the results provide some support for a verdict in favour of trade creation, they certainly do not rule out the opposite conclusion of trade diversion, in line with the conclusion of Adams *et al.*[55] The indication that ANZCERTA has resulted in a diversion of exports away from non-members is particularly strong. If the results of Adams *et al.* and DeRosa are considered together, the overall indication that ANZCERTA should be considered a trade diverting PTA is considerably stronger than in the case of major PTAs that were found by Adams *et al.* to be trade diverting, such as the European Union, NAFTA, MERCOSUR, and AFTA.

This is especially surprising, given that ANZCERTA was given the fourth highest score of all PTAs in the sample on Adams *et al*'s merchandise liberalization index and second highest score on their non-merchandise liberalization index. Nor does it square particularly well with the conventional view of ANZCERTA as one of the most far-reaching and comprehensive PTAs in terms of its liberalization processes. There is something of a puzzle here, which may offer an avenue for further research.

Implications for the welfare effects of ANZCERTA are perhaps even more unsettling. It was noted earlier that a PTA found to be trade diverting on a net basis must be welfare reducing. The results suggest that there is a not insignificant probability that this is the case with ANZCERTA. On the other hand, even if ANZCERTA were shown to be trade creating on a net basis, this would not guarantee that it must be welfare enhancing, as explained earlier.

Intra-Industry Trade

Intra-industry trade (IIT) under ANZCERTA is of interest both because it accounts for a substantial proportion of trans-Tasman trade in manufactures, and because intra-industry trade is often thought to be associated with lower adjustment costs, as noted earlier.

Using the well known Grubel-Lloyd index, the BIE found that the proportion of intra-industry trade is much higher in trans-Tasman trade than in trade with the rest of the world. They also found that growth of IIT in the "modified" sectors in the early years of ANZCERTA (to 1986–87) was particularly strong, although this appears to be at least partly due to changes in the balance of trade in these sectors. It was also noteworthy that growth of IIT in the "unaffected" sectors was similar to that in the "affected" sectors.

The BIE concludes from the evidence that liberalization under ANZCERTA encouraged both inter-industry and intra-industry trade. It also notes that the evidence appears to suggest that "there is a trend toward intra-industry trade in manufactures between Australia and New Zealand that is independent of the liberalization" taking place under ANZCERTA.

Menon and Dixon (1995) criticize the methodology used in earlier studies of intra-industry trade, which they consider leads to biased results, and develop a methodology designed to overcome the deficiencies that they identify. Using their methodology they found that trans-Tasman trade made very little contribution to the growth of the multilateral trade of each country, that intra-industry trade with New Zealand made only a small contribution to the change in the overall growth of Australia's IIT, but that intra-industry trade with Australia accounted for almost half of the overall growth in New Zealand's IIT. The latter result occurred despite the fact that Australia accounted for less than 5 per cent of the growth in New Zealand's total trade.

In the later 1986–91 period the significance of trans-Tasman intra-industry trade increased. Trade with New Zealand made a contribution to the overall growth of Australia's trade (almost 7 per cent of the total increase) that was slightly more than commensurate with New Zealand's share of Australia's trade, while intra-industry trade with New Zealand made a disproportionally large contribution to the growth of Australia's overall intra-industry trade, almost 18 per cent of the total increase of 165 per cent. In the same period trade with Australia accounted for just over a third of the total increase in New Zealand's trade (47 per cent), while intra-industry trade with Australia contributed almost half of the overall increase (74 per cent) in New Zealand's intra-industry trade.

Investment

Adams *et al.* (2003) use their methodology to estimate the effects of PTAs on investment flows, in this case covering the period 1988–97. For this purpose they use two sets of three PTA-specific dummy variables. In a manner analogous to the three PTA-specific dummies used in their analysis of trade effects, these dummies are intended respectively to capture changes in investment flows between members, changes in inward investment flows from non-members, and changes in outward flows to non-members. The dummies take on zero or non-zero values in the same manner as the dummies used to analyse trade. One set of three dummies is intended to capture the impact on investment of the trade provisions of the PTA, and the non-zero values for these dummies are taken from the MLI devised by Adams *et al.* The other set of dummies is intended to capture the effect on investment of the so-called "new age" or "third wave" provisions of the PTAs, and the non-zero values for these dummies are derived from those of the non-merchandise MLI. As in their analysis of trade effects Adams *et al.* perform estimations both with and without fixed effects.

Adams *et al.* note that the establishment of PTAs could have either positive or negative effects on investment, depending on the structure and motivation of both investment and intra-PTA trade. In relation to intra-PTA investment, the existence of the PTA could lead more firms to serve partner markets by trade rather than by investment, or it could stimulate intra-PTA investment by facilitating vertical integration within the PTA area by multinational firms. In relation to investment from non-members, there could be a "beachhead effect", with firms seeking to establish a presence in one of the PTA partners in order to serve the entire PTA area. There could also be an unwinding of earlier tariff jumping investment, with firms seeking to rationalize their investments within the PTA area now that investment is no longer necessary to gain access to each partner market. A combination of increased intra-FTA investment and increased inward investment from non-members could be indicative of a "beachhead" motive for investment. Increased outward investment to non-members might indicate a reversal of tariff jumping investment.

The results reported by Adams *et al.* indicate that trade provisions of PTAs generally have a weaker effect on investment than "new age" provisions. This is true of ANZCERTA as it is of most of the PTAs in the sample. In fact, as Table 8 shows, the trade provisions of ANZCERTA are estimated to have negatively affected investment in all directions, although most of the results are not significant, and Adams *et al.* in fact caution that their results for the investment effects of ANZCERTA are not reliable.

Table 8 also shows that "new age" provisions have a stronger impact on ANZCERTA investment flows, as they do for other PTAs in the sample. The effect on intra-PTA investment flows and on inward flows from non-members is again negative, but these

TABLE 8
Gravity Model Results for Investment Effects of ANZCERTA
(Adams *et al.* 2003)

Period: 1988–97
Tobit Maximum Likelihood Estimates

	Dummy 1 (Intra-PTA Trade)	Dummy 2 (Import Diversion)	Dummy 3 (Export Diversion)	Net Effect: Trade Creation (TC) or Trade Diversion (TD)
Trade Provisions				
w/o fixed effects	–3.780	–1.636	–3.376*	ID
with fixed effects	–6.503	–1.667	–2.352	–
"New Age" Provisions				
w/o fixed effects	–9.653	–6.506*	27.525***	IC
with fixed effects	–19.975*	–6.481**	29.245***	IC

Source: Author's compilation from various studies.

effects are outweighed by a strong positive effect on outward flows to non-members, so that the overall effect of the "new age" provisions is one of investment creation. Adams *et al.* do caution that the strong positive effect on outward flows to non-members could partly reflect other factors not controlled for in their model specification, for example, in Australia's case, the boost to its role as a capital exporter from financial deregulation and the growth of superannuation funds. It may also be relevant that ANZCERTA has not hitherto contained provisions for the liberalization of trans-Tasman investment, and that the investment regimes of both Australia and New Zealand have recently been assessed by the OECD as somewhat restrictive in certain aspects, as noted earlier (Koyama and Golub 2006).

10. Conclusion: Possible Lessons for ASEAN

This concluding section of the report briefly highlights some of the distinctive features of the process of economic integration between Australia and New Zealand, before going on to consider possible lessons for ASEAN.

In economic integration initiatives there is generally some combination of historical, geographical, political, institutional, and social factors that predisposes the participating countries towards integrating with each other and/or that facilitate the process of integration once it has begun. In the case of Australia and New Zealand these factors have included:

- Shared historical experiences and long-standing cultural ties;
- A sense of common geographical and political positioning within the wider surrounding region;
- Similarities in legal systems and regulatory approaches;
- Pre-existing labour mobility between the two countries; and
- Existence of federal/state institutional arrangements in Australia that could be extended relatively easily to New Zealand (covering, for example, government purchasing and mutual recognition).

Despite the factors favouring integration, progress has not been automatic. Significant initial difficulties had to be overcome before a "breakthrough" was achieved that firmly established the commitment to integration on both sides. The early "breakthrough" has been followed by alternating "progressive" and "flat" periods in the integration process.

The following are tentatively put forward as possible lessons for ASEAN from the ANZCERTA experience.

1. Strong political support at the leadership level has been vitally important in sustaining the momentum of the integration process. This has been especially true in propelling the process across important thresholds, such as the "breakthrough" represented by the 1988 Review, and subsequent periods of transition from "flat" to "progressive" periods in the process.

2. The pursuit in both countries of wide-ranging economic reform agendas, including strong commitments to unilateral trade liberalization, facilitated political acceptance of individual integration initiatives, which could often be presented as natural extensions of the domestic reform process.

3. The periodic setting by leaders of objectives for the integration process has been important. Objectives were specified in broad terms rather than as detailed "blueprints" and were accompanied by the establishment of processes of consultation, dialogue, review, and joint study that helped to sustain the momentum of the process in the succeeding years.

4. A strongly pragmatic approach was taken for the pursuit of the objectives, focusing on issues that were highlighted as important to the business sectors of both countries, or that were otherwise identified as impediments to integration for which practically and politically feasible solutions could be anticipated. Issues that were seen to raise severe political difficulties or sensitivities tended to be avoided, especially

if the economic pay-off from addressing them was not seen to be substantial.

5. A pragmatic approach was also taken to institutional development. Supranational institutions were avoided. Joint institutions were established where considered necessary or desirable to facilitate implementation of new initiatives that were agreed from time to time by the parties, rather than in accordance with any predetermined blueprint.

6. In the absence of a formal dispute settlement process, dispute resolution relies on consultative processes involving ministers and officials. This approach appears to be preferred by the parties and has generally worked reasonably well. There have been cases, however, where recourse to a robust dispute settlement process might have facilitated early resolution of issues which, in the event, continued as irritants to the relationship for many years.

7. Consultation with, and pressure from, the business sector in both countries was an important factor in prioritizing the steps to be taken in pursuing deeper integration. Pressure that emanated from the business sector in only one of the two countries was less successful in securing changes.

8. The potential for trade diversion and consequent resource misallocation arising from the necessarily discriminatory character of an agreement such as ANZCERTA has been a theme in several assessments of ANZCERTA by professional economists. Ongoing unilateral trade liberalization of MFN tariffs by both partners has significantly reduced the scope for such distortionary effects. Nevertheless, empirical research has not been able to establish definitively that ANZCERTA is a trade-creating rather than trade diverting FTA.

9. Even in countries with similar legal and regulatory systems, significant obstacles can be encountered in efforts to

harmonize or reach agreement on some important areas of policy and law.

10. Even in a well established integration process, external shocks can create new challenges in apparently settled areas of policy.

Notes

1   Officially known as the Basic Treaty of Friendship and Cooperation between Australia and Japan.

2   Holmes *et al.* (1986) set out a number of the issues that emerged in the early years of ANZCERTA. See also Scollay (1996).

3   This assessment is based in part on personal communication with officials involved in the 1988 Review.

4   Department of Treasury, Government of Australia; Invest Australia; Overseas Investment Office — New Zealand (2008).

5   Bondietti (2008).

6   Koyama and Golub, OECD (2006).

7   The Treasury of Australia (2006).

8   Prime Minister Kevin Rudd, Media Statement with NZ Prime Minister John Key 2nd March 2009.

9   Made under the AQA.

10 New Zealand Agriculture Ministry (2007).

11 World Trade Organization — Dispute Settlement: Dispute DS245 (2005) "Japan — Measures Affecting the Importation of Apples", available at <http://www.wto.org/english/tratop_e/dispu_e/cases_e/ds245_e.htm>.

12 New Zealand Agriculture Ministry (2007).

13 WTO (2009).

14 World Trade Organization. "Australia — Measures Affecting the Importation of Apples from New Zealand, Dispute DS367, Current status", 2010; available at <http://www.wto.org/english/tratop_e/dispu_e/cases_e/ds367_e.htm>.

15   Council of Australian Governments (2009), available at <http://
      www.coag.gov.au/mutual_recognition/tt_mutual_recog_agreement.
      cfm>.

16   New Zealand Ministry of Foreign Affairs & Trade (2008) "The Trans-
      Tasman Mutual Recognition Arrangement (TTMRA)", available at
      <http://www.mfat.govt.nz/Foreign-Relations/Australia/1-CER/0-
      ttmra.php>.

17   Mutual Recognition Act (Commonwealth) (1992).

18   Food Regulation Review Committee (1998) "Report of the Food
      Regulation Review", available at <http://www.foodstandards.gov.au/
      _srcfiles/2006_Final%20FRR%20(Blair)%20report.doc>.

19   Findlay and Round (2008).

20   Findlay and Round (2008).

21   Findlay and Round (2008).

22   Findlay and Round (2008).

23   Department of Infrastructure, Transport, Regional Development
      and Local Government, Australian Government (2009).

24   Knibb (2008) "What Next for Qantas", Flightglobal, available at
      <http://www.flightglobal.com/articles/2008/12/24/320510/what-next-
      for-qantas.html>.

25   Centre for Asia Pacific Aviation (2008) "Qantas Malaysia Airlines
      "merger" talks look like the real thing", available at <http://
      www.centreforaviation.com/news/2008/12/17/qantas-malaysia-
      airlines-merger-talks-look-like-the-real-thing/page1>.

26   Ionides (2009) "Australasian Airlines Confront Difficult Times",
      available at <http://www.flightglobal.com/articles/2009/03/02/323185/
      australasian-airlines-confront-difficult-times.html>.

27   Centre for Asia Pacific Aviation (2009) "Qantas Group Launches
      Full Frontal Attack on New Zealand", available at <http://www.
      centreforaviation.com/news/2009/02/18/qantas-group-launches-full-
      frontal-attack-on-new-zealand/page1>.

28   International Business Times. "Jetstar taxis to a head-on collision
      with Air NZ, adds more flights in New Zealand", 2010; available at

<http://www.ibtimes.com/articles/62717/20100916/jetstar-taxis-to-a-head-on-collision-with-air-nz-adds-more-flights-in-new-zealand.htm>.

[29]   Australian Government — Department of Immigration and Citizenship (2006) "Fact Sheet 17 — New Zealanders in Australia", available at <http://www.immi.gov.au/media/fact-sheets/17nz.htm>.

[30]   Australian Government — Department for Foreign Affairs and Trade (2008) "New Zealand Country Brief — November 2008", available at <http://www.dfat.gov.au/GEO/new_zealand/nz_country_brief.html>.

[31]   New Zealand Ministry of Foreign Affairs & Trade (2008) "CER: A Closer Economic Relationship", available at <http://www.mfat.govt.nz/Foreign-Relations/Australia/1-CER/index.php>.

[32]   WTO (2009).

[33]   Gretton and Gali (2005).

[34]   Australian Productivity Commission (2004) "Rules of Origin under the Australia-New Zealand Closer Economic Relations Trade Agreement Commissioned Study", available at <http://www.pc.gov.au/projects/study/roo/docs/finalreport>

[35]   Asia-Pacific Economic Cooperation (APEC), Senior Officials' Meeting (SOM) Policy Dialogue on Regional Trade Agreements (RTA), Free Trade Agreements (FTA), Khon Kaen, Thailand, 27 May 2003.

[36]   Australian Productivity Commission (2004).

[37]   Productivity Commission (2004).

[38]   Productivity Commission (2004).

[39]   Ultimate Customs Services Pty Ltd (2006) "New Rules of Origin ANZCERTA", Newsletter December 2006, and, Australian Customs Service (2006) "New Rules of Origin — ANZCERTA", Customs Notice No. 2006/64.

[40]   Consulate-General of New Zealand (2006) "Australia New Zealand Closer Economic Relations Trade Agreement", available at <https://www.fta.gov.au/default.aspx?FolderID=287&ArticleID=233>.

[41]   Australian Customs Service, (2009).

[42]   Ultimate Customs Services (2006) "Newsletter 2006/6 — New Rules of Origin-ANZCERTA", available at <http://www. dlr.com.au/ NEWSLETS/dlr1206.pdf>.

[43]   Australian Competition and Consumer Commission (2005) "ACCC Annual report 2004–2005", available at <http://www.accc.gov.au/ content/index.phtml/itemId/710675>.

[44]   ACCC & NZCC (2006) — "Cooperation Protocol for Merger Review".

[45]   While barriers other than tariffs can be important, in the interest of simplicity the following discussion focuses on tariffs.

[46]   This term is used to distinguish it from what is sometimes called gross trade creation, which refers to the total increase in intra-FTA trade, and includes the component that consists of trade diversion. Net trade creation is that part of the increased intra-FTA trade that does not consist of trade diversion.

[47]   This point becomes important when considering how to interpret the results of gravity models that focus on the amounts of trade created and diverted without being able to take the price differences into account.

[48]   Note that this definition of gross trade creation in the Truman model differs slightly from the definition given earlier.

[49]   DeRosa (2007) explains that the two "new" dummy variables introduced to capture import and export effects separately are also taken into account in assessing the overall effect of trade between the members of the PTA. This elaboration is omitted in the above explanation.

[50]   It may be of interest in the context of this report to note that AFTA is also included among the PTAs found to be trade diverting by Adams *et al.*

[51]   DeRosa augments Rose's dataset with data derived from the National Bureau of Economic Research (NBER).

[52]   In the case of sample of 46 PTAs DeRosa abandons the MLI index approach and reverts to the more conventional binary dummy

variable approach found in Soloaga and Winters (2001) and elsewhere.

[53] In truncated data, only non-zero trade flows are included.

[54] In censored data all trade flows equal to or less than US$10,000 are set equal to the natural log value of that figure (DeRosa 2007).

[55] Another recent study, by Jugurnath *et al.* (2007), employing three PTA-specific binary dummy variables, does find that the coefficients for all three dummy variables for ANZCERTA are positive. Their model is considerably less sophisticated than those of Adams *et al.* (2003) and DeRosa (2007). For example their sample includes only four PTAs plus one non-preferential arrangement (APEC).

References

Adams, R., P. Dee, J. Gali, and G. McGuire. "The Trade and Investment Effects of Preferential Trading Arrangements — Old and New Evidence". Productivity Commission Staff Working Paper, Canberra, 2003.

Anderton, Jim and Phil Goff. "NZ to take Australia to WTO over Apples Access". *Ministry of Agriculture and Ministry of Trade of New Zealand*, 2007; available at <http://www.bechive.govt.nz/release/nz+take+australia+wto+over+apple+access+0>.

Australian Competition and Consumer Commission. "ACCC Annual Report 1999–2000", 2000; available at <http://www.accc.gov.au/content/index.phtml/itemId/302720>.

———. "ACCC Annual report 2001–2002", 2002; available at <http://www.accc.gov.au/content/index.phtml/itemId/302705>.

———. "ACCC Annual report 2002–2003", 2003; available at <http://www.accc.gov.au/content/index.phtml/itemId/387849>.

———. "ACCC Annual report 2004–2005", 2005, available at <http://www.accc.gov.au/content/index.phtml/itemId/710675>.

———. "ACCC Annual report 2006–2007", 2007; available at <http://www.accc.gov.au/content/index.phtml/itemId/816120>.

———. "ACCC Annual report 2007–2008", 2008; available at <http://www.accc.gov.au/content/index.phtml/itemId/845735>.

Australian Competition and Consumer Commission and New Zealand Commerce Commission. "Cooperation Protocol for Merger Review", 2006; available at <http://www.accc.gov.au/content/item.phtm l?itemId=757826&nodeId=2f9a007f6ec97f492637b4afbe097458&fn= Cooperation%20protocol.pdf>.

Australian Government — Austrade. "Australia New Zealand Closer Economic Agreement (ANZCERTA) — An Overview", 2009; available at <http://www.austrade.gov.au/ ANZCERTA/default. aspx>.

Australian Government — Australian Customs Service. "New Rules of Origin — Australia New Zealand Closer Economic Relations Trade Agreement (ANZCERTA)" *Australian Customs Notice No. 2006/ 64*, 2009, 2006; available at <http://www.customs.gov.au/webdata/ resources/notices/acn0664.pdf>.

Australian Government — Department for Foreign Affairs and Trade. "New Zealand Country Brief — November 2008", 2008; available at <http://www.dfat.gov.au/GEO/ new_zealand/nz_country_brief. html>.

Australian Government — Department of Immigration and Citizenship. "Fact Sheet 17 — New Zealanders in Australia", 2008; available at <http://www.immi.gov.au/media/fact-sheets/17nz.htm>.

Biosecurity Australia. "Final Import Risk Analysis Report for Apples from New Zealand". *Press Release BA06/03*, 2006; available at <http://www.daff.gov.au/about/media-centre/dept releases/2006/ nz_apple_final_ira_report_media_release_-_30_november>.

———. "Import Risk Analyses Handbook 2007", 2007; available at <http://www.daff.gov.au/__data/assets/pdf_file/0011/399341/ IRA_handbook_2007_WEB.pdf>.

———. "Biosecurity Policy Determination — Importation of Apples from New Zealand, 27 March 2007", 2007; available at <http://www. daff.gov.au/_ data/assets/pdf_file/0006/176523/2007-07.pdf>.

————. "Import Risk Analysis Report for Apples from New Zealand Appeal Findings, 26 February 2007 Findings of IRA Appeal Panel", 2007; available at <http://www.daff.gov.au/__data/assets/pdf_file/0011/155387/2007_04.pdf>.

————."Biosecurity Australia Policy Memorandum Notifying the Release of the Final Import Risk Analysis Report for Apples from New Zealand, 30 November 2006", 2006; available at <http://www.daff.gov.au/__data/assets/pdf_file/0005/100022/2006_37.pdf>.

————. "Final IRA Report for Apples from NZ — Part A", 2006; available at <http://www.daff.gov.au/__data/assets/pdf_file/0006/100023/2006_37a.pdf>.

————."Final IRA Report for Apples from NZ — Part B", 2006; available at <http://www.daff.gov.au/__data/assets/pdf_file/0007/100024/2006_37b.pdf>. '

————."Final IRA Report for Apples from NZ - Part C", 2006; available at <http://www.daff.gov.au/__data/assets/pdf_file/0008/100025/2006_37c.pdf>.

————."Eminent Scientists Group Report on the NZ Apple IRA to the Director of Animal and Plant Quarantine", 2006; available at <http://www.daff.gov.au/__data/assets/pdf_file/0010/100027/ESG_NZapples.pdf>.

Bjorksten, N. "The Current State of New Zealand Monetary Union Research". Reserve Bank of New Zealand Bulletin 64 (4), (2001): 44–55.

Bondietti, K. "Inconsistencies in Treatment of Foreign Investment in Trade Agreements". Australian APEC Study Centre, Monash University December 2008, 2008; available at <http://www.apec.org.au/docs/08_AASC_IFDI.pdf>.

Bureau of Industry Economics. "Trade Liberalisation and Australian Manufacturing Industry: The Impact of the Australia-New Zealand Closer Economic Relations Trade Agreement", *AGPS* (Australian Government Publishing Services): Canberra, 1989.

————. "Impact of the CER Trade Agreement: Lessons for Regional Economic Cooperation", *AGPS*.: Canberra, 1995.

Centre for Asia Pacific Aviation. "Qantas Group Launches Full Frontal Attack on New Zealand", 2009; available at <http://www.centre foraviation.com/news/2009/02/18/qantas-group-launches-full-frontal-attack-on-new-zealand/page1>.

———. "Qantas Malaysia Airlines "Merger" Talks Look Like the Real Thing", 2008; available at <http://www.centreforaviation.com/news/2008/12/17/qantas-malaysia-airlines-merger-talks-look-like-the-real-thing/page1>.

Consulate-General of New Zealand. "Australia New Zealand Closer Economic Relations Trade Agreement", 2006; available at <https://www.fta.gov.au/default.aspx?FolderID=287& ArticleID=233>.

Crean, Simon and Phil Goff. "2008 CER Ministerial Forum Joint Statement", Ministry of Trade of Australia and New Zealand, 2008; available at <http:// www.trademinister.gov.au/releases/2008/sc_cer_joint_communique.html>.

Crosby, M. and G. Otto. "An Australian New Zealand Currency Union", in de Brouwer, G. (ed.), Financial Markets and Policies in East Asia.: Routledge, 2002.

Department of Foreign Affairs and Trade. "Closer Economic Relations: Background Guide to the Australia New Zealand Economic Relationship". Canberra, 1997.

Department of Infrastructure, Transport, Regional Development and Local Government, Australian Government. "The Open Skies Agreement", 2009; available at <www.infrastructure.gov.au>.

DeRosa, D. "The Trade Effects of Preferential Arrangements: New Evidence from the Australian Productivity Commission". Working Paper WP 07-1, Peterson Institute for International Economics.: Washington D.C., 2007.

Findlay, Christopher C. and David K. Round. "Competition Policy in International Airlines Markets: An Agenda and a Proposal Solution". Paper prepared for the conference on Comparative Experience in Competition Policy Reform: Australia, Japan and East Asia. Canberra: Australian National University, 22–23 September 2008.

Food Regulation Review Committee. "Report of the Food Regulation Review", 1998; available at <http://www.foodstandards.gov.au/srcfiles/2006Final% 20FRR%20(Blair)%20report.doc>.

Food Standards Australia New Zealand. "Imported Food", 2003/2009; available at <http://www. foodstandards.gov.au/newsroom/factsheets/ factsheets2003/ importedfoodinspecti1985.cfm>.

Frankel, J. "Regional Trading Blocs in the World Economic System". Institute for International Economics, Washington D.C. 1997; available at <www.fta.gov.au>.

―――. Australian Free Trade Agreement "Australia New Zealand Closer Economic Relations Trade Agreement — Rules of origin", 2007; available at <https://www.fta.gov.au/ default.aspx?FolderID=287& ArticleID=233>.

Gali, J and P. Gretton."The Restrictiveness of Rules of Origin in Preferential Trade Agreements". Australia: Productivity Commission Canberra, 2005.

Gilbert, J., R. Scollay and B. Bora. "New Regional Trading Arrangements in the Asia-Pacific Region". In *Global Change and East Asian Policy Initiatives*, World Bank, Washington D.C. edited by S. Yusuf, N. A. Altaf and K. Nabeshima (2004): 190–121.

Government of New Zealand. "Information on Social Security benefits for Australians Living in New Zealand", 2002; available at: <http://executive. govt.nz/minister/clark/australia/information2.pdf>.

Grimes, A. "Regional and Industry Cycles in Australasia: Implications for a Common Currency". *Journal of Asian Economics* 16 (2005): 01–18.

Grimes, A., F. Holmes and R. Bowden. "An ANZAC Dollar? Currency Union and Business Development". Institute of Policy Studies, Wellington, 2000.

Holmes, F. *et al.* "Closer Economic Relations with Australia: Agenda for Progress", Institute of Policy Studies, Wellington, 1986.

Hudson, Andrew. "Still Setting the Agenda", Hunt & Hunt — LIV International Law Section Newsletter Jan/Feb 2009, 2009; available at <http://www.hunthunt.com.au/pageSys/ DocView.aspx? DocumentID=2140>.

Hunt, C. "A Fresh Look at the Merits of a Currency Union". Reserve Bank of New Zealand Bulletin 68(4), (2005): 16–30.

Ionides N. "Australasian Airlines Confront Difficult Times", Flightglobal & Airline *Business*, 2009; available at <http://www.flightglobal.com/ articles/2009/ 03/02/323185/australasian-airlines-confront-difficult-times.html>.

Jugurnath, B., M. Stewart and R. Brooks. "Asia/Pacific regional Trade Agreements: An Empirical Study". *Journal of Asian Economics* 18, (2007): 974–87.

Key, John and Kevin Rudd. "Statement on Trans-Tasman Cooperation". Media Statement 2 March 2009. Available at <http://www. beehive.govt.nz/ release/joint+statement+strengthened+ns-tasman+cooperation>.

———. "Joint Statement on Strengthened Trans-Tasman Cooperation Commonwealth Parliamentary Offices, Sydney". *Interview*, 2009; available at <http://www.pm.gov.au/media/Interview/2009/ interview0846 .cfm>.

Kissling, C. "Beyond the Australasian Single Aviation Market". Australian Geographical Studies 36 (2), (July 1998): 170–76.

Knibb, David. "What Next for Qantas". Flightglobal & Airline Business, 2008; available at <http://www.flightglobal.com/articles/2008/12/24/ 320510/what-next-for-qantas.html>.

Koyama, T. and St. Golub. "OECD's FDI Regulatory Restrictiveness Index: Revision and Extension to more Economies". Working Paper on International Investment Number 2006/4, 2006; available at <http://www.oecd.org/dataoecd/4/36/37818075.pdf>.

Lee, J-W. and I. Park. "Free Trade Areas in East Asia: Discriminatory or Non-discriminatory?". *World Economy* 28, no. 1 (2005): 21–48.

Li, Q. "Institutional Rules of Regional Trade Blocs and their Impact on International Trade", In *The Political Consequences of Regional Trade Blocks*, edited by R. Switky and B. Kerremans. Ashgare, London (2000): 85–118.

Lloyd, P.J. "The Future of CER: A Single Market for Australia and New Zealand", Committee for Economic Development of Australia and Institute of Policy Studies, Melbourne and Wellington, 1991.

————. "The Future of Trans-Tasman Closer Economic Relations". *Agenda* 2, no. 3 (1995): 267–80.

Lloyd, P.J. and L. L. Song. "A Currency Union between Australia and New Zealand". *Economie Internationale* 107, (2006): 149–72.

Menon, J. and P. B. Dixon. "Regional Trading Arrangements and Intra-Industry Trade: The Case of ANZCERTA". General Paper no. G-114, Centre of Policy Studies and the Impact Project, Melbourne, 1995.

Ministry of Economic Development. "Existing Vehicles for Trans-Tasman Institutional Cooperation", 2007; available at <http://med.govt.nz/ templates/Multi pageDocumentPage_30313.aspx>.

Ministry of Foreign Affairs and Trade. "Key CER Instruments", 2008; available at <http://www.mfat.govt.nz/Foreign-Relations/Australia/ 1-CER/0-cer-timeline.php>.

————. "The Australia New Zealand Closer Economic relations (CER) Trade Agreement: 1983–2003 Backgrounder", 2008: available at <http://www.mfat.govt.nz/Trade-and-Economic-Relations/0-Trade-archive/0-Trade-agreements/Australia/0-trade-agreement.php>.

————. "The Single Economic Market Agenda", 2009; available at <http://www.mfat.govt.nz/Foreign-Relations/2-SEM/index.php>.

New Zealand Commerce Commission. "Commerce Commission Annual Report 2004–2005", 2005; available at <http://www.comcom.govt.nz/ /Publications/ ContentFiles/Documents/Annual%20Report%202004-2005%20-%20web0.pdf>.

————. "Commerce Commission Statement of Intent 2005–2006", 2005: available at <http://www.comcom.govt.nz// Publications/Content Files/ Documents/SOI%202005_2006.pdf>.

————. "Commerce Commission Statement of Intent 2006–2009", 2006; available at <http://www.comcom.govt.nz//Publications/Content Files/Documents/SOI%202006-07.pdf>.

————. "Commerce Commission Statement of Intent 2007–2010", 2007; available at <http://www.comcom.govt.nz//Publications/Content

Files/Documents/COMCOM%20SOI%202007_2.pdf>.

———. "Commerce Commission Statement of Intent 2008–2011", 2008: available at <http://www.comcom.govt.nz//Publications/Content Files/Documents/SoI%202008-11.pdf>.

New Zealand and Australian Governments, New Zealand Ministry of Foreign Affairs & Trade. "The Single Economic Market agenda", 2008; available at <http://www.mfat.govt.nz/ Foreign-Relations/ Australia/2-SEM/index.php>.

———. CER: A closer economic Relationship", 2008; available at <http://www.mfat.govt.nz/Foreign-Relations/Australia/1-CER/ index.php>.

———. "Key CER Instruments", 2008; available at <http://www. mfat.govt.nz/Foreign-Relations/Australia/1-CER/0-cer-timeline.php>.

———. "The Australia New Zealand Closer Economic relations (CER) Trade Agreement: 1983–2003 Backgrounder", 2008; available at <http://www.mfat.govt.nz/Trade-and-Economic-Relations/0-Trade-archive/0-Trade-agreements/Australia/0-trade-agreement.php>.

———."The Trans-Tasman Mutual Recognition Arrangement (TTMRA)", 2008; available at <http://www.mfat.govt.nz/Foreign-Relations/ Australia/1-CER/0-ttmra.php>.

New Zealand Press Association. "Air NZ 'disappointed' by BA Qantas deal". *Business and Finance, The West Australian*, 2008; available at <http://origin-www.thewest.com.au /aapstory.aspx?StoryName =534820>.

Ochia, R, Philippa Dee and Christopher Findlay (2009), "Services in Free Trade Agreements". In *Free Trade Agreements in the Asia Pacific, World Scientific*, edited by Christopher Findlay and Shujiro Urata. Singapore, 2009.

Productivity Commission. "Evaluation of Mutual Recognition Schemes". Productivity Commission, Canberra, 2003.

———. "Rules of Origin under the Australia New Zealand Closer Economic Relations Trade Agreement". Productivity Commission, Canberra, 2004.

———. "Review of Mutual Recognition Schemes". *Productivity Commission*, Canberra, 2009.

Power, Simon. "Single Economic Market discussions in Australia". New Zealand Government, 2009; available at <http://www.beehive.govt.nz/rele ase/single+economic+mark et+discussions+australia>.

Radio New Zealand. "New Zealand to take Australia to WTO over Apple Ban", 2007; available at <http://www.nowpublic.com/new-zealand-take-australia-wto-over-apple-ban>.

Reuters. "NZ takes Australia to WTO over Apple Import Rules", *ABC News*, 2008; available at <http://www.abc.net.au/news/stories/2008/01/11/2137001.htm>.

Rose, A.K. "Do We Really Know that the WTO Increases Trade? (*American Economic Review* 94, no. 1 (March 2004): 98–114.

Sandilands, Ben. "Qantas-BA=Why not have another crack at Air New Zealand?", *Plane Talking*, 2008; available at <http://blogs.crikey.com.au/plane talking/2008/12/19/qantas-bawhy-not-have-another-crack-at-air-new-zealand/>.

Scollay, R. "Australia-New Zealand Closer Economic Relations Agreement". In *Regional Integration and the Asia-Pacific*, edited by B. Bora and C. Findlay. Oxford University Press, Melbourne, 1996.

Scollay, R., W. Friesen, N. Haworth and R. LeHeron. "Death of an Industry: The New Zealand Motor Industry Fails to Survive Free Trade". paper presented at Thai APEC Study Centre Conference on "Impact of APEC on Domestic Affairs", Bangkok, 27–28 August 1998.

Shewan, J. "Tax Harmonisation". In *CER and Business Competition*, edited by K. Vautier, J. Farmer and R. Baxt. Commerce Clearing House, Auckland, 1990.

Soloaga, I. and L. A.Winters. "Regionalism in the nineties: What effect on trade". *North American Journal of Economics and Finance*, 12 no. 1 (2001): 1–29.

Tang, D. "Effects of the Regional Trading Arrangements on Trade: Evidence from the NAFTA, ANZCER and ASEAN Countries, 1989–

2000". *Journal of International Trade and Development* 14, no. 2 (2005): 241–65.

Thomson, G. "A Single Market for Goods and Services in the Antipodes". *World Economy* 18 no. 2 (June 1989): 207–18.

Ultimate Customs Services. "Newsletter 2006/6 — New Rules of Origin-ANZCERTA", 2006; available at <http://www.dlr.com.au/NEWSLETS/dlr1206.pdf>.

Vautier, K.M. and P. J. Lloyd. "International Trade and Competition Policy: CER, APEC and the WTO". *Institute of Policy Studies*, Wellington, 1997.

Welfarerights.org. "Social Security payments for New Zealand citizens living in Australia", 2009; available at <http://www.welfare rights.org.au/Factsheets/ fsssnz.doc>.

World Trade Organization. "Australia — Measures Affecting the Importation of Apples from New Zealand (DS367)", 2008; available at <http://www.wto.org/ english/tratop_e/dispu_e/cases_e/ ds367_e.htm>.

———. "Australia — Measures Affecting the Importation of Apples from New Zealand, Communication from the Chairman of the Panel, Preliminary Ruling by the Panel". WT/DS367/7, 2008.

———. "Australia — Measures Affecting the Importation of Apples from New Zealand, Communication from the Chairman of the Panel". WT/DS367/8, 2008.

———."Australia — Measures Affecting the Importation of Apples from New Zealand, Constitution of the Panel Established at the Request of New Zealand, Note by the Secretariat". WT/DS367/6, 2008.

———. DISPUTE SETTLEMENT: DISPUTE DS245. "Japan — Measures Affecting the Importation of Apples", 2005; available at <http:// www.wto.org/ english/tratop_e/dispu_e/cases_e/ds245_e.htm>.

Yamarik, S. and S. Ghosh. "Does Trade Creation Measure Up? A Reexamination of the Effects of Regional Trading Arrangements". *Economics Letters* 82 (2004): 213–19.

———."A Sensitivity Analysis of the Gravity Model". *International Trade Journal* XIX, no. 1 (2005): 83–126.

ABOUT THE AUTHORS

Robert Scollay is associate professor of economics and director of the APEC Study Centre at the University of Auckland in New Zealand. He has researched and written extensively on regional economic integration issues, as well as other trade policy issues, with special emphasis on developments in the Asia-Pacific region.

Christopher Findlay is professor and head of the School of Economics at the University of Adelaide. His research interests include Australia's economic relationships with Asia. He is an active participant in the network of the Pacific Economic Cooperation Council. Work in progress includes assessment of barriers to trade and investment in services.

Uwe Kaufmann is a PhD candidate at the School of Economics, University of Adelaide. His research interests are international trade and the impact of free trade agreements. Currently he is investigating the utilization of Australia's free trade agreements and the impacts of a potential Australian (and New Zealand) free trade agreements with the Pacific Island Countries (PACER Plus).